# Don't Touch My Heart

## HEALING THE PAIN OF AN UNATTACHED CHILD

*Lynda Gianforte Mansfield and
Christopher H. Waldmann, MA, LPC*

D1125626

PIÑON PRESS

P.O. Box 35007, Colorado Springs, Colorado, 80935

Library of Congress Catalog Card Number:
94-5508
ISBN 08910-98208

Cover and interior illustrations: Jonathan
Weast

Mansfield, Lynda Gianforte.
    Don't touch my heart: healing the pain
of an unattached child / Lynda Gianforte
Mansfield and Christopher H.
Waldmann.
        p.   cm.
    Includes bibliographical references.
    ISBN 0-89109-820-8
    1. Attachment behavior in children.
2. Problem children—Case studies.
3. Children psychotherapy—Case
studies. 4. Maternal deprivation—Case
studies. I. Waldmann, Christopher H.
II. Title.
RJ507.A77M36 1994
618.92'89—dc20                    94-5508
                                        CIP

Printed in the United States of America

*To Ty and Kelly—*
*our greatest inspiration,*
*our greatest challenge,*
*our greatest joy*

# FOREWORD

Pain. Loss. Neglect. And abuse. They are piled upon developing infants while their small brains develop. Neurons are being laid down, and essential connections are hard wired. The early environment is imprinted on their memories, affecting the way they will live their lives forever.

Little monkeys raised in captivity cannot even figure out how to handle a swaying tree branch, so they fall out when put in the wild. Dogs beaten in infancy are forever ferocious and nontrusting. What the environment gives young mammals—any mammal—the adult then offers the world.

Increasingly, the environment is giving loss and abuse to human infants. Inevitably, early loss leads to rage. The rage felt toward the abandoning parent is projected onto adoptive parents and future love relationships, and it is ultimately expressed hatefully onto society itself.

This story about Jonathan is typical. Typically sad. A young mother who is unable to complete high school—who is unable to form any lasting or meaningful relationship— is nevertheless one of the hundreds of thousands who is paid, per baby, to continue to reproduce. As the infants, like Jonathan, grow to the age when they can assert themselves, their inadequate parents abandon them to the public system.

But the general public ordinarily does not have to witness infantile pain. As a result, the issue is largely ignored— leaving institutions, foster parents, and adoptive parents to cope with the problems posed by children who grow increasingly dangerous as they grow older. Yes, the violence given infants happens in the privacy of dysfunctional and violent homes. But these children grow up and leave the privacy of their homes, and their inner violence is then projected in a distressingly more public way.

A fifteen-year-old shoots a fourteen-year-old because the

younger child won't kiss his feet. An infant in a city park zoo is gunned down. Killing takes the lives of more children than illness or suicide. Drive-by shootings and car-nappings threaten all city dwellers at night. Whatever happened to love? Where does all the hate come from? These are the questions posed by the average American.

And this book has the answers.

*Don't Touch My Heart* lucidly and movingly documents both the causes of severe disturbance in childhood and the outcome. It illuminates the fact that without therapy, Jonathan—although adopted into a loving and high-functioning home—could easily have developed into a lonely, loveless, and threatening public menace.

*Don't Touch My Heart* clearly, completely, compellingly, and concisely clarifies the strange and almost incomprehensible symptoms and responses of the character-disturbed child. It demonstrates how the typical and inadequate "usual treatment methods" have no hope at all of getting through. It tells of the more harsh—but ultimately more loving—methods that *do* reach the child and help the family.

It is a book that every thinking American concerned with America's increasingly disturbed youth should read.

Foster W. Cline, MD
*Founder, Evergreen Consultants in Human Behavior*
*Founder, The Attachment Center at Evergreen*

# ACKNOWLEDGMENTS

We have dedicated this book to our children, Ty and Kelly, who allowed us to touch their hearts. We sadly embraced their lives pre-therapy; we joyously celebrate the lives that emerged post-therapy.

It is because of these children that we had a story to tell. As it began to unravel, we enlisted the aid of many people. We are grateful for the expertise of Dr. Foster Cline, into whose hands we thrust an early, unfinished manuscript. We thank DeOnne Noel, LCSW, and Liz Randolph, PhD, whose professional knowledge helped shape our tale. A very special thanks goes to Jill Row who always listened, who never failed to understand, and whose sensitive observations provided new depth and tenderness to our story.

We are indebted to our talented illustrator, Jonathan Weast, who endured more information about attachment disorder than he ever wanted to know. Particular recognition goes to our agent, Mike Hamilburg, a true man of honor. We thank Nancy Burke, whose warmth and compassion provided our first introduction to the Piñon family. Heartfelt appreciation goes to Traci Mullins, who entered our lives as an editor and settled comfortably there as a friend.

Most importantly, we are grateful to our families—a constant source of unwavering support and belief in this project. To Tom, Ty, and Marcus . . . to Peggy, Kelly, and J. Chris . . . we thank you for enduring our absences and distractions.

And lastly, we thank each other—for the contributions that we brought to the book from our individual perspectives, for the mutual encouragement that saw us through the final chapter, and for the rewards of a steadfast friendship.

# PROLOGUE

Imagine being so consumed by rage that you are compelled to destroy everything in your world. Imagine feeling such primitive fury that your behavior becomes more animalistic than human. Imagine enduring these emotions and being only five years old.

This is the life of the unattached child—a child who, during infancy, does not bond to a primary caregiver. Bonding, or attachment, is a critical part of a child's development because it affects his or her ability to form close, trusting relationships throughout life.

A break in the bonding cycle is best illustrated by the diagram below:

SOURCE: *Understanding and Treating the Severely Disturbed Child,*
*Foster W. Cline, MD*

*As perhaps the most helpless creature on earth, the newborn infant must rely entirely on an external source to fulfill his basic needs . . . food, physical comfort, and loving contact. He expresses these needs through rage—pure, simple, primitive rage. When he cries, this rage is ideally gratified by a primary caregiver who feeds him, changes him, rocks him, smiles at*

9

*him. The rage is satisfied, and he learns to trust. Later in life, this trust translates to a willingness to accept limits and controls imposed by his parents and other authority figures.*

*When the cycle is broken—specifically at the point between expression of rage and gratification—so is the vital connection to the outside world. Without the necessary input of eye contact, touch, motion, lactose, and smiles, a bond does not take place. Instead of learning that he can depend on someone else to meet his needs, the infant gets the message that he can trust no one but himself. Control becomes a major issue and is directly related to his ultimate concept of survival.*

When we consider that nearly half of everything a person will learn in a lifetime is learned during the first year of life, we can begin to understand how critical the messages received in infancy are to future development.

All of our society's children can fall victim to attachment disorder. It is not exclusive to those born into poverty. It is not confined to foster children and adopted children. It can happen to any child, anywhere in the world. And it is happening every day.

There are a variety of conditions that place a child at risk for attachment disorder. They include:

▶ Physical, emotional, or sexual abuse
▶ Neglect
▶ Sudden separation from the primary caregiver
▶ Undiagnosed and/or painful illness
▶ Prenatal abuse, including drugs and alcohol
▶ Frequent foster placements and/or failed adoptions
▶ Inconsistent or inadequate child care
▶ Mother's prolonged absence, either physical or psychological
▶ Lack of environmental stimulation
▶ Protein malnutrition or other organic problems that affect brain functioning

**SOURCE: *Dr. Foster Cline***

10

Surprisingly, most children who suffer from attachment disorder exhibit similar personality traits. In his book *Understanding and Treating the Severely Disturbed Child*, Dr. Foster Cline outlines seventeen common warning signs:

1. Superficially engaging and charming
2. Lacks eye contact on parental terms
3. Indiscriminately affectionate with strangers
4. Not affectionate on parents' terms (not cuddly)
5. Destructive to self, others, and material things (accident prone)
6. Cruel to animals
7. Lies about the obvious (crazy lying)
8. No impulse control (frequently acts hyperactive)
9. Learning lags
10. Lack of cause-and-effect thinking
11. Lack of conscience
12. Abnormal eating patterns
13. Poor peer relationships
14. Preoccupation with fire
15. Persistent with nonsense questions and incessant chatter
16. Inappropriately demanding and clingy
17. Abnormal speech patterns

Some of these symptoms carry more weight than others. For instance, most unattached children are superficial and have a nonexistent or underdeveloped conscience. These pathologies will therefore stand out when the child exhibits them. If seven or more of the seventeen symptoms are present, parents should consult a qualified professional who is familiar with the diagnosis and treatment of attachment disorder.

Children who are depressed, who are experiencing an adjustment reaction to changes in life—such as moves or divorce—or who have experienced unresolved trauma—such as a death in the family or sexual abuse—will also act out many or all of these symptoms. Consequently, it is

11

crucial to weigh the symptomatology against historical factors relating to the child's background in order to arrive at an accurate diagnosis.

In *Don't Touch My Heart* we explain the far-reaching social implications of attachment disorder through the life of Jonathan Jacob Justice, a child who was born into an abusive environment. Written for both adults and children, the book chronicles Jonathan's young life through a series of foster placements, eventually following him into an adoptive home. Here we reveal Jonathan's inner struggles and secrets. We unmask his terrifying awareness that he is "different." And we share the pain he imposes on his new family, particularly his adoptive mother.

Since Jonathan did not bond in infancy as a result of his early abuse, he has difficulty giving and receiving love. His response to others is based on fear and uncertainty, and because he has been conditioned not to trust anyone but himself, he believes he must maintain control of all situations in order to survive.

Sadly, our nation has given birth to hundreds of thousands of children like Jonathan. If left undiagnosed and untreated, these children will grow up to impose their bruised and damaged psyches on their families. On their friends. On their co-workers. And on total strangers.

Sometime during our lives, we will all cross paths with attachment-disordered individuals. They might charm us. They might con us. They might shock us with unconscionable cruelty. They are the face of our future, and it is a frightening face.

Appropriate intervention is necessary if the cycle of abuse breeding abuse is to be broken. We as parents, educators, social workers, therapists, and law enforcement and legal professionals must learn to recognize the voice that cries out for help. For acknowledgment. For understanding.

Responding appropriately to that voice does not come naturally. It does not come easily. It is a unique and sensitive intervention that requires training and cultivation to meet the special needs of these special children.

*Don't Touch My Heart* explores the benefits of holding therapy, a highly effective technique that teaches a child that giving up control can help him or her to experience love and trust instead of abuse and abandonment. It is one approach to the problem of attachment disorder; there are others, but we do not address them here.

In most instances, holding therapy takes place in a series of ten daily, three-hour intensive sessions that occur over the course of two weeks. The length of treatment depends on the severity of the child's disorder and his response to therapy. Sometimes, it is recommended that a child stay with therapeutic foster parents during these intensives.

The intervention of holding therapy is not a cure. It is not a "quick fix." It is the first step in changing the child's world—releasing the rage that must be freed before any emotional rebuilding can take place. A combination of strong parenting skills, continued therapy, and a solid relationship with teachers all contribute to the child's healing process.

Our fictional account of Jonathan's experience with the therapy is typical of most attachment-disordered children. Others are more resistant and do not respond as quickly or as well. In any case, it is perhaps the only chance these children have of moving into the future free of the constraints of their dysfunctional early lives.

And when they are free, we all are free.

Jonathan Jacob Justice lives in a rambling old
farmhouse
    with doors that creak
    and floors that slope
    and windows that stick
    and dogs that lick
    and cats that purr
    and people who laugh.
    A lot.

    He has a dad who tickles
    and a mom who cuddles
    and a brother who teases
    and a sister who giggles.
    A lot.

    There's a backyard swing
    and a rabbit in a hutch
    and a hole in the fence
    and a hose that leaks.
    A whole lot.

All these things and all these people are part of
Jonathan's world—a world very, very different from
the one he used to know.

♥

Jonathan was born seven years ago in a place far
away from the farmhouse. He never knew his birth
dad, and his birth mom didn't know very much
about how to take care of a baby. She left him alone

a lot of the time. She also did drugs a lot of the time, and to Jonathan, that was the same as being left alone. When he cried, she didn't pick him up and hold him. Instead, she screamed at him to stop, but of course Jonathan didn't understand the words. Sometimes, she ignored him, which was even worse than the screaming. Even though Jonathan was just a baby, he was beginning to understand that he couldn't depend on this mom for anything at all.

♥

One day, when Jonathan was almost three years old, his birth mom took him to her friend Annie's house. Annie's house was the place she sometimes went when the job of being a mom was just too hard for her.

"I need you to watch him for a few hours," she said. "I'll be back by 6:00 tonight."

When 6:00 came, Jonathan's birth mom didn't. When 9:00 came, she still wasn't there. When the sun came shining through the windows the next morning and she still wasn't there, Jonathan felt dark clouds move into his heart.

When he began to cry, Annie hit him. When he cried even harder, Annie hit him again. She called the police and told them to take Jonathan away. The police called Children's Protective Services, and soon a social worker was knocking on Annie's apartment door.

The social worker's name was Laura. She smiled at Jonathan, but he was afraid. She sat him on her lap, and he was even more afraid. Jonathan didn't like grownups. In fact, Jonathan didn't like anyone at all.

♥

Laura took Jonathan from Annie's apartment, and soon he was living in a foster home. There were five other children living there, too, and Jonathan didn't like it one bit.

He screamed at the other children, just like his birth mom had screamed at him. And he hit the other children, just like Annie had hit him.

Jonathan felt angry inside, so he shouted as loudly as he could to try to shout the anger away. He punched as hard as he could to try to punch the anger away. And he kicked as swiftly as he could to try to kick the anger away. But the anger stayed with him, just like a close friend.

Jonathan's foster parents tried very hard to be patient with him, but they worried that he would seriously hurt one of the other children. His behavior became worse and worse, and when he was four years old, they finally asked the social worker to take him away.

♥

This time Laura took him to a home where a kindly, older couple lived. Their children were all grown up, and Jonathan was the only little boy in the house. He wanted very much for these new foster parents to like him, so he buried his anger deep inside and smiled his sweetest smile.

17

Jonathan was on his best behavior with his new family. He called them Nanna and Poppa, just like they asked him to. He made his bed every morning, and always remembered to put his toys away. He fed the fish—but not too much—and helped with the dishes without being asked. He cuddled with Nanna and Poppa whenever they wanted, and he always said "please" and "thank you."

One bright, sunny day Laura came to visit him. "I have a surprise for you," she said in a smiling voice. "We're going to play in the park today!"

Jonathan grabbed his jacket and followed her out the door, remembering at the very last minute to kiss Nanna and Poppa goodbye.

When they arrived at the park, Laura led Jonathan to the swings. And there, on the end swing—the blue one with the chipped paint—sat his mother.

Jonathan hesitated at first, then ran straight into her arms. She cried as she held him, but soon they were laughing and playing together. It had been more than a year since they'd seen each other, but her smell and her touch were familiar and comfortable.

It seemed much too soon when Laura said it was time to go. She promised him that he would see his mother again. His mother promised, too. And Jonathan thought it was the happiest day of his life.

♥

A week later, Nanna started packing Jonathan's belongings. She cried while she did it, and Poppa kept wiping his eyes with the back of his hand.

Jonathan didn't care that they were unhappy. He knew he was going home to his mother, and that was all that mattered to him.

When he heard Laura's car, he ran outside. He yanked the car door open and climbed inside, and he never even said goodbye to Nanna and Poppa.

The ride seemed to take forever, but they finally stopped in front of a brick apartment building that Jonathan had never seen before.

"This is where your mom lives now," Laura said. "This is your new home."

Jonathan dashed up the steps as fast as he could. Laura caught up to him and ran her finger down a long row of doorbells before selecting one. Jonathan could hear footsteps on the stairs inside, and soon his mother was opening the front door.

She picked him up and hugged him tightly, then led Laura up the stairs and down a long hallway. Her apartment was at the end, and had a small number "6" on the door. The three of them went inside, and sat at the kitchen table drinking lemonade and eating cookies. Jonathan's mother smiled at him a lot, and it made him feel special.

When Laura left, Jonathan and his mom moved into the small living room to watch cartoons. Jonathan didn't even care what was on television. He was back with his mom, and his world was good.

♥

For the next few weeks, Jonathan and his mother spent all their time together. No one came to visit,

19

and they never went to visit anyone.

Then one day, a dark-haired man with a shaggy mustache came to the door. Jonathan's mother called him Pete, and she was very happy to see him. Jonathan could tell that she liked Pete a lot, because she kept kissing him and telling him how much she missed him.

"Who's the kid?" Pete asked, as he jerked his thumb at Jonathan.

"Oh, I'm babysitting for a friend," Jonathan's mom replied nervously, as she led Pete into the bedroom and slammed the door.

Jonathan stared at the closed door, feeling his chest grow tight. His thoughts swirled in his head like snowflakes in a snowstorm, as he tried his best to figure out what was happening. *Why didn't his mom tell Pete who he was? Why did this man seem so important to her?* The more he thought, the farther away the answers seemed to be.

♥

Jonathan was still feeling hurt and confused when Pete came out of the bedroom.

"Come here, kid," he said to Jonathan, as he sat on a living room chair. He pulled Jonathan onto his lap, and began to hug him and stroke him in ways no one had ever done before. He touched Jonathan in private places, and the feelings were good-bad feelings that confused him. Nanna and Poppa had taught him that touching this way was bad, but if it was bad, why did it feel kind of tingly-good?

20

When Jonathan's mother came out of the bedroom, Pete quickly pushed the little boy off his lap. More confused than ever, Jonathan ran up to her and tried to climb into her arms.

"Don't! You'll get me dirty!" she cried, grabbing his wrists and yanking his smudged hands away from her. She then turned sweetly to Pete, softening her voice as she spoke to him. "How about that dinner you promised me?" she asked him.

"Let's go," he replied, and the two of them walked toward the door.

"We won't be long," Jonathan's mother said to him, talking over her shoulder. "We'll bring you back something to eat," she promised. And then they were gone.

♥

Jonathan didn't know what to do. He tried to watch television, but the happy family on the screen made him feel angry. He tried to draw a picture, but all he could make were jagged, black scribbles. He watched the sun go down, and the apartment was filled with long, gray shadows. Jonathan pretended that the shadows were monsters, who would pounce on his mother and Pete when they returned.

But soon the shadows were gone, and darkness replaced them. Jonathan turned on a lamp, then wandered into the kitchen. He felt hungry and very much alone. The hunger and the loneliness combined to create a deep, empty space inside him, and he began to open cupboard doors in search of

something to fill the emptiness.

He found a large bag of sugar on a top shelf, and climbed onto the counter to reach it. Pulling it down, he plunged his hand deep inside and came up with a fistful of soft, sweet granules. He sat on the floor and began to eat them, closing his eyes and gently rocking as he licked every trace of the sugar from his fingers.

The more Jonathan ate, the better he felt. The sugar took away his hunger. It took away his loneliness. And it took away his emptiness—but only for a little while.

Jonathan was asleep on the kitchen floor when his mother and Pete came home. Their loud laughter awakened him, and at first he didn't know where he was. Soon the laughter turned to shouting, and before long the apartment was vibrating with the sound of their angry voices. Jonathan crawled under the table and curled up into a ball, covering his ears to block the noise.

Jonathan didn't know how much time had passed, but suddenly a policewoman was picking him up from his hiding place.

"It's a good thing the neighbor called us because of the commotion," he heard the woman say. "Who knows what those two might have done to this poor kid."

Jonathan looked up and saw a policeman searching through his mother's purse. He drew out a small plastic bag, and inside was something that looked just like sugar. Jonathan had a sudden urge to be eating sugar again right now, and the feeling was so strong he could almost taste the sweetness.

"Cocaine," the policeman said, as he sampled a tiny bit of the substance in the bag. He then told Pete to empty his pockets, and Pete looked very much afraid. He pulled out a tattered wallet and some loose change. He pulled out a crumpled tissue and a small knife. Then he pulled out a plastic bag, and it looked just like the one from Jonathan's mother's purse.

Before Jonathan could figure out what was happening, the policeman had put handcuffs on his mother and Pete and was leading them away.

*The shadow-monsters got them after all,* Jonathan thought, as he let his head drop on the policewoman's shoulder.

♥

Jonathan spent the rest of the night at the police station, and when morning came, so did Laura. She took him straight to Nanna and Poppa's house, and they were overjoyed to have him back.

"We missed you, little one," Nanna said kindly, and when she spoke, he knew he had to change back into the sweet child she remembered. And he did—just like that.

♥

The days passed quickly and were filled with picnics, visits to the zoo, and a thrilling day at the amusement park. Jonathan continued to act like a perfectly behaved child, and kept all his secrets hidden away.

It wasn't long before Nanna and Poppa decided to send Jonathan to preschool. He was almost five years old—and they felt that he was ready. They found one that they especially liked right nearby, and they enrolled him in a class with twenty other children. There were four long tables in the room, with little chairs that were just the right size. On the very first day, Jonathan crawled under one of the tables and refused to come out.

"I don't belong here," he cried. "I don't belong anywhere!"

He scratched the teacher when she tried to console him, and he growled at the other children when they peered at him curiously. He felt like a wild animal in a cage, so that's how he acted. He stayed under the table during snack time and nap time, and he didn't come out until it was time to go home.

When Nanna came to pick him up, she was shocked at the news the teacher gave her. Jonathan was such a good boy at home, she couldn't believe he was acting so badly at school.

"Perhaps he just needs to get used to a new place," she said to her husband that night, long after Jonathan had been put to bed.

"Yes, that must be it," he agreed, and they both went to sleep hoping they were right.

♥

As the weeks went by, Nanna and Poppa knew that they were wrong. Jonathan refused to take part in class projects. He refused to play on the playground.

25

He even refused to make any friends at all. Anger was now Jonathan's best friend—locked in a secret place inside him, a place that only he could reach.

At home, Jonathan still appeared to be a pleasant child. But the closer Nanna and Poppa looked, the more they began to realize that there was something not-quite-right about his pleasantness. When he smiled at them, the brightness never reached his eyes. When he hugged them, his touch felt cold. And when he said "I love you," the words sounded hollow and empty.

Before long, they began to feel that Jonathan was a stranger to them. Although they loved him as deeply as if he were their own child, their love didn't seem to be reaching him. This made them sad. It made them so sad that they didn't want to live that way anymore.

♥

It was a crisp fall day when Poppa called Laura on the phone. "Jonathan seems so empty," he said. "He says and does all the right things, but they just don't *feel* right. It's as if he's keeping his real feelings locked away.

"This is very painful for us," he went on to say, "but we'd really like you to come and take Jonathan away."

Laura drove up to the house a few hours later. Jonathan was standing by the window, and he watched as she walked up to the front door. Laura was the one person who had been a part of his life

26

longer than anyone else. He knew that whenever Laura appeared, it meant that he would disappear— from his home, from his foster parents, and from everything that had become familiar to him.

Nanna and Poppa cried when he left. But Jonathan never cried. His tears and his real feelings were tucked away in that faroff place that belonged to him alone.

Laura looked across at Jonathan as they drove away. He stared straight ahead, clutching his canvas suitcase to his chest. She wondered to herself why he seemed so unfeeling. She wondered why he didn't cry. She tried to talk to him, but Jonathan didn't seem to have anything to say.

Soon they arrived at the children's receiving home. It was a very big place, with lots of open space outside and lots of noisy children.

"This is where you'll stay for a while," Laura said to Jonathan, "until we can find you a new home." She introduced him to the director—a small, smiling woman named Mrs. Miller—and then she was gone.

♥

Mrs. Miller escorted Jonathan upstairs to a room that he would share with three other boys. It was a crowded room, with four narrow beds in the middle and four squat dressers along the walls. She showed him which bed and dresser would be his, then told him to unpack his things.

"I'll be waiting downstairs, dear," she said to Jonathan. "Please come down when you're finished, and I'll introduce you to some of the children."

Jonathan stuffed his few belongings into his dresser and kicked his suitcase under his bed. He gazed around the room, and his eyes came to rest on a large cork bulletin board that was mounted near the window. Someone—Mrs. Miller, perhaps, or maybe the boys who lived here—had pinned magazine photographs all over it. There were pictures of puppies and horses, flowers and butterflies, race cars and rocket ships. There were sailboats and motorcycles, clowns and cowboys, tigers and seagulls.

Jonathan didn't know why, but seeing those pictures made him angry. In fact, the more he looked, the angrier he became. He began tearing at the photographs—slowly at first, then faster and faster and faster until nothing was left but tiny pieces of paper that floated around his feet and scattered across the floor. Jonathan looked down at the colorful scraps, and a smile crept across his face.

♥

When Jonathan went downstairs, he found Mrs. Miller in the kitchen. Two tall boys, much older than Jonathan, were sitting at a long, scuffed table eating apples and raisins and drinking milk.

"Come join us, dear," said Mrs. Miller, as she poured a glass of milk for Jonathan. "I'd like you to meet Robert and Sam," she said, and the boys looked at him and smiled. "This is Jonathan, our new friend," she went on, as she placed her arm

29

protectively around Jonathan's shoulders.

Jonathan was suddenly unable to stand Mrs. Miller's touch, and he pulled away roughly. "I'm not their friend," he said angrily. "I'm not anybody's friend!" he shouted, and he ran back to his room where he stayed for the rest of the day.

♥

**A** month went by, and then Laura came to visit. She brought chocolates for Jonathan, and he munched them on the back porch while Laura met with Mrs. Miller in the kitchen.

"I just can't find any foster parents who'll take him," he overheard Laura say. "He's such a difficult child, and no one is willing to put up with his disruptive behavior." She sighed sadly then, and her sigh was like a floodgate that opened up, letting rage pour into Jonathan's heart.

He ran around to the front of the house and let himself in through the heavy oak door. He raced up to the second floor and dashed into his room. He threw himself down on his bed and punched at his pillow. He felt angry and afraid and hurt, all at the same time. Suddenly he sat up straight, as if a great thought had struck him.

"I'm a big boy now," Jonathan said, in a voice that was barely a whisper. "I'm five years old, and I don't need a special home to take care of me. I don't need a mother, and I don't need a father. I can take care of myself just fine."

Leaving his suitcase and his few possessions

behind, Jonathan tiptoed down the stairs and walked quickly and quietly out the door.

♥

This was a strange neighborhood to Jonathan, but that didn't matter to him. He just walked and walked. And even though he didn't know where he was going, he didn't care.

The street was a busy one, with lots of traffic racing in both directions. He heard honking horns and screeching brakes, and the noises excited him. Once he even heard a siren, and the sound made him shiver with delight. Jonathan hoped that the siren was from a fire truck, and that a huge fire was raging out of control somewhere in the city. He imagined people being hurt in the fire, and he thought that would be good.

Right in the middle of these thoughts, a police car pulled up to the curb. It startled Jonathan, and he stopped in his tracks as if frozen to the spot. A tall man with hair the color of flame climbed out and walked up to where Jonathan was standing.

"Hi there, big guy," the policeman said cheerfully. "A fine day for a walk, isn't it?"

"Oh, I'm so glad you found me!" Jonathan cried suddenly, as he threw himself into the policeman's arms. "I had to run away from that terrible place, and I had nowhere to go!"

"Just calm down," the policeman soothed, as he gently held Jonathan. "My name is Officer Ryan, and I'm here to help you."

He eased Jonathan into the back seat, then listened as the little boy told his story. Jonathan wove an elaborate tale about his experiences at the receiving home. He told Officer Ryan about the big boys, Robert and Sam, and he sobbed when he said that they crept into his room at night and touched him in private places.

He described the things that Pete had done, but he blamed them on Robert and Sam.

Officer Ryan drove straight to the receiving home and knocked on the front door. Mrs. Miller rushed to open it, with Laura close behind.

"I found this child wandering down Twelfth Street," he announced in a deep voice. "He told me that he lives here."

"Oh, Jonathan!" Mrs. Miller cried, as she reached down to hold him. "We didn't know where you'd gone!"

Jonathan wriggled out of her grasp and directed his words to Officer Ryan, ignoring Laura as he did so. "I told them both what Robert and Sam did to me," he said miserably, "but they wouldn't listen."

Mrs. Miller looked at Jonathan in astonishment, and Laura stepped forward and stood beside him as he continued.

"Please don't let those boys touch me again, Officer Ryan. Please don't let them do those horrible things to me."

"What do you think we should do about this?" Officer Ryan asked, addressing his question to Laura. "You certainly can't keep the child here."

"I'll take him to my office," said Laura. "I can handle things from there. Thank you for your help," she concluded, and the policeman nodded and left.

Jonathan grinned to himself as he clutched Laura's hand and walked to the car, never once looking back. Getting Robert and Sam in trouble made him feel powerful. It made him feel important. And it made him feel very, very special.

♥

Laura took Jonathan straight to her office. She gave him some toys to play with, then sat down wearily at her desk. She thought about Jonathan's claim that he had been abused by Robert and Sam. Although he sounded convincing, she wasn't quite sure if he was telling the truth. Laura had known Robert and Sam for several months, and abuse seemed out of character for their personalities and their backgrounds. But until she could be sure, she had to find another home for Jonathan immediately.

She thought of the Justices, a new foster family she had met the day before. Although they had requested a child younger than five, they might consider taking Jonathan if they understood the urgency of moving him out of the receiving home. She called them right away, and they agreed to let her bring Jonathan to their home that afternoon.

"Jonathan, I have some important news to tell you," Laura said, looking at him intently. Jonathan simply stared at the smudges on her glasses, but he knew that she would think he was looking straight into her eyes.

"I'm going to take you to stay with some very

nice people," she said, and he was not surprised. He was beginning to feel like a package that was lost in the mail. Every time it showed up at a new post office it turned out to be the wrong post office, and the package had to be shipped off again. Nobody claimed it. Nobody wanted it. And that was just how Jonathan felt.

When Laura took him to his next foster home, they were greeted at the door by a man and a woman who were introduced as Dan and Susan. Dan was very tall, with broad shoulders and bright blue eyes that crinkled at the corners when he smiled. Susan had long dark hair and dark eyes, and she reminded Jonathan of an Indian princess.

They welcomed him warmly, and invited him to meet their children. Nicholas was seven, and had very proper manners. He shook hands with Jonathan, and Jonathan thought that was pretty dumb for a kid. Hayley was almost three, and she was chubby and pink-cheeked and babbling.

*Just like a girl,* Jonathan thought contemptuously, as he walked past them all and entered the living room.

♥

**A**s Jonathan plopped down on the sofa, a change came over him that no one could see. And no one could feel. In fact, no one knew what was happening at all. No one, that is, except Jonathan.

Slowly, very slowly, he pushed his anger and frustration deep down inside himself. He put a smile on his face, and looked up at his new foster family.

"Thank you for letting me live with you," he said in his most charming voice. "I'm sure I'll be very happy here."

Dan and Susan looked at each other and smiled. Then Susan sat on the sofa beside Jonathan and gave him a gentle squeeze.

"We're happy to have you, Jonathan," she said. "We want you to feel like a part of our family."

Jonathan returned Susan's hug. "Oh, thank you!" he said aloud, but inside he said, *This is going to be easier than I thought.*

♥

**A**s the days and weeks passed, Jonathan convinced Susan and Dan that he was the perfect child. He called them Mom and Dad now, and they always looked pleased when he did.

Things were going so well, in fact, that Susan and Dan made the decision to adopt Jonathan. His young life had been such a difficult one, and they believed they could provide him with the love and attention he needed to grow into a happy, secure child. He always seemed so polite. He always seemed so eager to please.

But whenever they weren't looking, a very different Jonathan emerged.

One day, when Jonathan was in the garden with Hayley, he decided to teach her a new game. "Let's play flower shop," he said. "You pick all the flowers, and I'll sit here and make them into beautiful

35

bouquets for Mom."

Hayley clapped her hands with joy, because she loved new adventures. She was eager to start the game, so she dutifully obeyed her new big brother. She picked tulips and daffodils. She picked irises and daisies. She picked lilies and violets and lilacs and pansies. Soon she had picked nearly all the flowers in the garden, and she happily delivered them to Jonathan in huge armfuls.

"Mom!" Jonathan squealed, as Hayley dropped the last bundle of flowers beside him and sat down in the midst of them. "Mom, come see what Hayley did to your beautiful garden!" he shouted, as he jumped up and ran toward the house.

In no time at all, he returned to the garden with Mom. There they found Hayley, surrounded by dozens of flowers, and much too confused even to cry.

"Look what she did, Mom!" Jonathan said in a horrified voice. "All your hard work—ruined!" he went on, and his shock and dismay sounded very convincing.

"I'm surprised at you, Hayley," Mom said sternly. "You know better than to pick the flowers."

Hayley wanted to explain to her mother what had really happened. She wanted to tell her that the game was Jonathan's idea, that he had told her to pick the flowers. But all she could do was take big gulps of air, and the words she tried to say made no sense at all.

"Hayley, go take a timeout in your room right now," Mom said, as she began gathering up the blossoms. "I'll decide on a consequence after dinner."

Hayley started to cry as she left the garden.

When she walked past Jonathan, she glared at him accusingly through her tears. Jonathan glared back, a wicked grin distorting the corners of his mouth. He muttered something very softly—so softly that only Hayley could hear.

"I'm in charge," he said menacingly. "From now on, things are going to go *my* way."

♥

Jonathan felt very proud of himself because getting Hayley in trouble was so easy. His next task was to do the same to Nicholas, but that would be harder because Nicholas was older.

Jonathan's chance came purely by accident one afternoon when he and Nicholas were alone in the barn sorting glass bottles for recycling. Dad had set up three large bins—one for clear glass, one for green glass, and one for brown glass. The boys were pitching bottles into the bins, and Nicholas was pretending to be a famous baseball player.

Impulsively, Jonathan grabbed the neck of a bottle and smashed it against the edge of one of the bins. The bottle shattered into pieces, leaving a large cut on his hand. Jonathan started to scream. He clutched his bleeding hand and ran into the field where Dad was mowing.

"Dad, Dad!" he shrieked, "Nicholas hurt me. He hurt me badly!"

He ran into his foster father's arms, squeezing big, fat tears out of the corners of his eyes. "We were sorting the bottles," he cried, "and I broke one by accident. Nicholas got mad at me and cut me with the broken glass."

"He's lying, Dad," Nicholas said. "I didn't do it—honest!"

Jonathan began to cry more dramatically, forcing loud sobs from deep inside his chest. "He hurt me because he hates me, Dad. He doesn't want me to live here. He doesn't want to share his family with me."

Jonathan cried and cried, clutching Dad tightly and sounding as if his heart were breaking. He could tell by the way Dad was hugging him that he believed Jonathan's story.

"Nicholas," Dad said, "you're on restriction for the rest of the week. And if you ever hurt your brother again, you'll lose all your privileges for a month. Now finish sorting those bottles by yourself. I'm going to tend to Jonathan's hand."

Nicholas pleaded his innocence once again, but his father wouldn't listen. His full attention was focused on Jonathan, whose face was still filled with the most intense sadness. But as Nicholas walked away, Jonathan buried his face in his father's shoulder. And smiled.

♥

Jonathan thrived on causing problems for Nicholas and Hayley. Every time he succeeded in getting one of them in trouble, he considered it a personal victory. He still managed to keep his negative behavior a secret from Mom and Dad, and he was very proud of that.

One bright autumn morning—when the leaves were beginning to turn color and the air held just a hint of crispness—Jonathan, Nicholas, and Hayley were playing tag in front of the house. Polo, one of the family's dogs, was romping in the grass with them.

Polo was a two-year-old labrador retriever. He was a very large dog, and he bounded and bounced around the yard with endless energy and enthusiasm. He was eager to be part of the children's game, and he ran after each of them with his ears flapping.

When it was Nicholas's turn to be "it," Jonathan dashed away from him as fast as he could. Polo dashed right after him, crossing in front of Jonathan's path and knocking him to the ground. Jonathan was stunned rather than hurt, but he lay there long enough for Nicholas to tag him. Polo stood close by, wagging his tail and waiting for the action to continue.

Jonathan was furious at having been knocked down. He was even more furious at being tagged. And he was convinced that it was all Polo's fault. He reached for the chain around the dog's neck, slipping his finger through the loop on the end of it. This made the chain pull tight around Polo's throat, and within seconds the dog began to choke. Jonathan kept tugging harder and harder, screaming at Polo as he did so.

Mom came running out of the house when she heard the noise, and she immediately pulled Jonathan away from the dog. Polo started breathing normally as soon as he was freed, and he licked Mom's face to say thank you.

Jonathan, on the other hand, was not so grateful to see her.

"Polo tried to bite me, Mom," he said in his defense. "I was just trying to get him away from me."

"That's not true! That's not true!" Nicholas and Hayley said in unison. They were sure that their mother would believe Jonathan, because it seemed that she always believed Jonathan. But this time, things were different.

"I know that Polo is a gentle dog," Mom said. "He would never try to bite anyone. Now, Jonathan, I want you to go to your room and do some thinking. Think about why you hurt the dog. And think about why you lied to me."

Jonathan muttered under his breath as he walked away. Getting caught misbehaving was not part of his plan.

When Dad came home from work that night, Mom told him what had happened.

"I'm worried about Jonathan," she said. "His behavior today seemed so filled with anger."

"There's no need to be concerned," said Dad. "Polo wasn't hurt, and Jonathan was just being a little rough. Don't make a big deal out of it."

But Mom thought it was a big deal. And she continued to worry.

♥

Two weeks later, when the incident with Polo was just a dim memory, the family began to plan for Jonathan's sixth birthday party. He was very excited,

41

because he'd never had a real birthday party before. When he lived with his birth mom, he never even knew when his birthday was. And when he lived in his first foster home, they didn't celebrate his birthday at all. Nanna and Poppa had a small party for just the three of them when Jonathan turned four—and the people at the receiving home gave him another small party when he turned five—but this would be a real celebration.

There would be lots of children and balloons and party favors and cake and ice cream and candy. There would be games and prizes and presents and music and even a clown to entertain the children. Jonathan thought he would burst with excitement, and he could hardly wait for the following Sunday.

Finally, the afternoon of Jonathan's party arrived. Ten children were invited, and they all brought presents wrapped in brightly colored paper.

The clown showed up in a little car painted like a rainbow, and her wild, fluffy hair was rainbow-striped to match. She had a red nose the size of a plum and a glittery bow tie that sparkled with shiny stars.

Her name was Melody, and she delighted the children with songs and puppet shows and balloon animals. She played the guitar and painted their faces and told wonderful tales about giant butterflies.

The hours flew by in a flurry of fun and activity, and soon it was time for Jonathan to open his presents. He sat in the middle of the living room floor, and Nicholas and Hayley took turns handing him the packages.

42

Jonathan could hardly believe the treasures that he received! There was a dinosaur with red eyes that flashed, and a fire truck with a siren that really worked. There was a picture book about trains and planes, and a paper mobile of all the planets. There were games and cards and videos and building things and just about everything a six-year-old boy could want.

Jonathan tore open each gift as fast as he could, then reached eagerly for the next one. Soon all of his birthday presents were unwrapped, and he sat back in a pile of wrapping paper, boxes, and ribbon.

"Is that all there is?" he asked in a very soft voice, but only Mom heard him.

Soon the children's parents began to arrive, and one by one the guests left the party. Jonathan remembered to thank each of them and to hand out small gift bags of candy.

When the last child said goodbye, Jonathan picked up his presents and took them to his room. He stayed there a very long time, then Mom finally went in to check on him.

Jonathan was sitting on the floor in the corner, and all his birthday gifts were lying in a broken, jumbled heap beside him. Everything—the dinosaur, the fire truck, the picture book, the mobile, the games, the cards, the videos, the building things— had been destroyed.

"Why, Jonathan, why did you do this?" Mom asked him, shaking her head sadly.

But Jonathan just looked at her and would not, could not, answer.

44

♥

"I think we should take Jonathan to a psychologist," Mom said to Dad, after she explained what Jonathan had done to his presents. "That kind of destruction just doesn't seem normal," she continued.

"I don't think there's any cause for alarm," Dad replied, "but if you think it's necessary, go ahead."

Mom went straight to the phone and called a friend of hers who was a teacher in the local elementary school. "I need the name of a good child psychologist," she said. "Can you help me?"

Her friend gave her the name of a woman who sometimes worked for the school—a psychologist who had an office nearby. Mom called her the very next day and made an appointment for Jonathan to see her the following Wednesday.

Mom was a bit nervous about the session, but Jonathan seemed very calm. The woman introduced herself as Dr. Moran, and Jonathan shook her hand politely. The three of them talked for a few minutes, and Jonathan's mom told the doctor about the birthday party. After a while, Dr. Moran said she wanted to spend some time alone with Jonathan.

Mom went out to the waiting room, and Dr. Moran closed the door to her office.

"Now tell me, Jonathan," she said, "how do you like living with your new family?"

"It's really a fun place," Jonathan began. "It's a big old farmhouse, and there's lots of animals and lots to do. I like to play with Nicholas and Hayley,

and Dad gives me piggyback rides to bed at night."
He smiled brightly as he made this little speech,
then frowned and hesitated slightly before continuing. "Mom acts kinda funny sometimes though," he
said in a worried voice. "She watches everything I
do, and when I make even a little mistake she gets
really mad."

Jonathan walked across the office and stood
beside Dr. Moran's chair. "I don't think she'll ever
love me as much as she loves Nicholas and Hayley,"
he said sadly, climbing into the doctor's lap. "I want
her to love me—I do, I do!" he cried, sobbing bitterly.

Dr. Moran stroked his hair until he had calmed
down, and then she took him by the hand and
walked him to a room where there were lots of toys.
"Wait here for a few minutes," she said to him. "I'd
like to talk to your mom."

She brought Jonathan's mom back into her
office and closed the door once again.

"Jonathan appears to be a perfectly normal little
boy," she began. "He probably destroyed all his
birthday presents because the excitement of the
party overstimulated him. If you could just learn to
relax and take things in stride, everything would be
fine. Just treat him the way you treat your other
children. Give him lots of love and attention, and
you'll find that you'll all be a lot happier and more
settled."

Jonathan's mom thanked Dr. Moran and agreed
to set up a schedule of weekly therapy sessions for
Jonathan. The two of them were silent as they left
the office and walked to the car, each lost in their

own thoughts. Mom had a sad look on her face, but Jonathan was smiling his smug little smile.

♥

In the months that followed, Mom did everything she could think of to make sure that Jonathan felt loved and happy. She baked his favorite cookies— peanut butter chocolate chip. She read his favorite books, and she played his favorite card games. She did his chores for him when he fussed, and she always helped him with his homework.

They did lots of things all by themselves, because Mom thought that would make Jonathan feel especially loved. They went to the movies. They went to the playground. And they went on long walks in the woods nearby. They gathered rocks and feathers, and once they found an Indian arrowhead. They continued to meet with Dr. Moran once a week—sometimes they talked to her together, and sometimes they talked to her alone.

♥

One day, shortly before Christmas, Dr. Moran called Mom into her office after a session with Jonathan.

"I see great improvement in him," she said. "Although there are still signs of restlessness and opposition, I believe he's really trying to fit in. No additional therapy sessions seem to be needed at this point. Just continue to do what you've been doing to make Jonathan feel that he's special to you, and I'm sure he'll settle in comfortably."

As Mom listened to Dr. Moran, her expression changed from surprise to delight. Although she didn't feel that Jonathan's behavior had improved significantly, she was pleased to hear that Dr. Moran thought so.

On the way home, she stopped at the bakery and bought Jonathan the gooiest, chocolatey-est cupcake she could find. As he bit greedily into the icing she watched him carefully, wondering if she would ever truly understand this little boy.

♥

Understanding Jonathan seemed to be an increasingly difficult task. Whenever Mom began to get a glimpse of what motivated him, he would do something completely to the contrary.

Early one afternoon, when Jonathan and Nicholas were still at school and Hayley was at play group, there was an unexpected knock at the front door. When Mom answered it, she was faced by a tall, slender man who identified himself as Greg North.

"I'm with Children's Protective Services," Mr. North said. "We've received an allegation of child abuse against you regarding your son Jonathan."

Mom felt as if she had been knocked to the ground. Her entire body began to tremble, and for a moment she was unable to speak. She motioned Mr. North into the living room, then sat down across from him.

"I . . . I don't know what you're talking about," Mom stammered, not knowing what else to say.

Mr. North crossed his legs and smoothed the crease of his trousers. His gestures seemed so casual—so out of place—that Mom felt a spark of anger mingle with her fear.

"Jonathan says you're not feeding him, Mrs. Justice," Mr. North began. "He told his teacher that you never give him lunch money, and that you often send him to bed without dinner. When his teacher suggested that she call you to confirm his story, he became hysterical. He begged her not to contact you, claiming that you would beat him for telling on you. That's when she called me. I must admit he was very convincing, Mrs. Justice. He was still sobbing when I arrived at the school, and his terror seemed genuine."

Mom's fear continued to give way to anger, and she stood up abruptly. "Mr. North," she said, "I've heard just about all I'm willing to hear. I have never deprived Jonathan of food, and I have never threatened to beat him. He's a troubled child, and he obviously made up the entire story. You're welcome to talk to my husband—to my other children—to anyone who knows us. I'm sure they can provide some honest insight," she added, an edge of sarcasm tinging her voice.

"I've tried everything I can to make things right for Jonathan," she sighed, sitting down once again. It's as if he feels the need to distance himself from the rest of the family, and his accusation fills that need. It almost seems that he doesn't *want* to be a part of us," she concluded, and her sadness filled the room.

Mr. North felt Mom's sadness and was touched by it. He thought about the hysterical little boy in the school office—the child certainly did not appear to be malnourished. He looked at the woman whom Jonathan claimed to fear—he couldn't picture her threatening a small boy. The pieces didn't fit together for him, and he made a decision on the spot.

"Mrs. Justice, I'm going to file an unsubstantiated report on this claim," he said. "At this point, I have no reason to believe that Jonathan's story is true. His teacher will, however, be keeping a close eye on him, and I'll be back if there's any additional cause for concern."

He stood to leave, and Mom walked him to the door. Although she felt relieved, she could begin to feel the tension building once again. She said goodbye quickly, then ran to the phone to call her husband at work.

Dad rushed home as soon as he received her call. He found Mom pacing in the kitchen and approached her with his arms outstretched. As he placed his hands on her shoulders, as he listened to her story, he saw that her eyes were colored by a new weariness, a new pain. At that moment, he realized he would have to find the strength for both of them, and he felt an overwhelming wave of resentment toward Jonathan. This child—this small child whose life they were trying to save—was systematically chipping away at their own lives.

When Jonathan came home from school, Mom and Dad confronted him about his accusations.

"I'm sorry I made up those lies," he confessed immediately, trying his best to put a contrite expression on his face. "I don't know why I did it, Mom—honest, I don't," he went on. "Can you forgive me?"

Mom became enraged at Jonathan's phony attempt at an apology.

"Don't you see—you could have destroyed our entire family!" she scolded, her voice rising with every syllable. "Get to your room—get away from me now!"

Jonathan turned and walked away, hiding the grin that flashed across his face. He felt giddy with power. Making Mom crazy was such an easy thing to do.

♥

Mom's fear of further allegations of child abuse subsided with each passing day. She continued to do special things just for Jonathan in the hope of drawing him into the family. She cooked the meals that he liked best—even broccoli and rice soup, which everyone else thought was terrible. But Jonathan loved it, so Mom made it—often twice in the same week.

She tried as hard as she could to help Jonathan fit in, but despite what Dr. Moran had said, nothing seemed to work. He was still mean to Nicholas and Hayley, but now he didn't even try to hide it. He was rude to everyone he met, and his school work began to suffer. It seemed that the more Mom tried to please Jonathan, the worse his behavior became.

Jonathan lied all the time. He lied about big things. He lied about little things. And he lied about obvious things. One day he even lied about sneaking some of Mom's baking chocolate, even though it was smeared all over his face.

Jonathan liked to steal food. Sometimes, late at night, he would climb out of bed and tiptoe into the kitchen. Without turning on any lights, he would make his way to the pantry and pull down the bag of sugar. Jonathan loved sugar, and he would sit on the floor of the pantry and eat big handfuls of it until sleepiness drove him back to his bed.

Jonathan liked to steal other things, too. He stole money from Mom's purse. He stole gum from Dad's dresser. He stole drawing paper from Nicholas and crayons from Hayley.

He stole things that he already had. He stole things that he didn't need. He stole things that he couldn't use, and he didn't know why.

♥

The more Jonathan's mother tried to help him, the more he misbehaved.

He broke the arm off Hayley's doll.

He lost three of Nick's chessmen.

He smashed a window in the kitchen.

He let the rabbit out of the hutch, and it was three days before they found her.

He searched through Mom's dresser drawers,

and hid one of her bracelets and a pair of her earrings. He hid them so well, in fact, that no matter how hard everyone looked, no one could find them.

With each passing day, Mom lost more and more patience with Jonathan. The more she learned about him the less she seemed to like him, and she felt guilty because she wasn't a very good mom to him. She wanted to love him the way she loved Nicholas and Hayley, but no matter how hard she tried, the love would not come.

In place of the love was a growing anger.

She became angry when he teased the cat.

She became angry when he played with his food.

She became angry when he wouldn't do his homework.

She became angry when he smiled his smug little smile.

She became angry when he acted in sneaky ways.

And sometimes she became angry over nothing at all.

♥

As Mom's anger increased, so did her frustration. It made her tense. It made her impatient. And it made her very, very sad.

One rainy Tuesday—when the sadness clung to her and would not let go—she called her friend Jill on the phone.

"Can you meet me for lunch today?" Mom asked. "I really need to talk to a friend."

When Jill said yes, Mom felt a brief spark of

relief. Jill was her closest friend, and sharing thoughts and feelings with her always came easily.

They agreed to meet at a little café in the center of town, and Mom arrived a few minutes early. She picked out a table along the back wall of the restaurant, beside a window that offered a view of the rain-spattered garden.

*I'm just like those flowers,* she told herself, watching the wind and water drive unceasingly at the delicate petals. *When the sadness comes—like the rain—there's no shelter, there's no peace. There's just a constant pounding that bears down on me, and my only choice is to ride the storm. I'm not sure of the outcome—will I survive it, or will I break and be tossed to the wind?*

She looked away from the window then, and discovered Jill standing beside the table. A small smile—the first in a long time—brightened Mom's face, and she stood to hug her friend. After they exchanged hellos and small talk—after they ordered their lunches—Mom's manner grew serious once again.

"I have a problem that I need to share with you, Jill," she began, nervously playing with her spoon. "I'm afraid there's something very wrong with Jonathan, and my feeling on this is more intense than anything I've ever known. When I look at him, I don't see a little boy at all. Instead I see a small, manipulative person who frightens me. When I look into his eyes, it seems as if he's staring into my very soul. His gaze is so intense . . . so terrifying, that I have to look away. I know this sounds crazy, but I'm actually afraid of him."

Where Mom expected to see compassion and understanding in the face of her friend, she now saw only annoyance and weariness.

"I really thought I knew you, Susan," Jill said, placing her fork on her plate with a slight clang, "but this is a side of you I've never seen before. I can't believe you actually think that Jonathan is a disturbed little boy. Just because you're having trouble dealing with him, you've convinced yourself that somehow it's his fault. I'm amazed that you're blaming a child for your own inability to cope. And let's face it, Susan—I spend a lot of time with your family. Surely if there were something really wrong with Jonathan, I'd see it, too. But I don't see anything—not a thing."

Jill reached across the table and took her friend's hand.

"I don't want to hurt you, Susan," she said, "but I think you're the one with the problem. You're obsessed with believing that Jonathan is an evil child, and it's causing you to overreact to things. You're so tense when you're around him, it's no wonder he misbehaves. Please—for your own sake—try to get a grip on things. He's just a little boy, not a monster. Give him a chance."

Jill's words stung Mom like a sudden slap. She had been certain that her friend would understand her feelings, but instead she was being blamed for Jonathan's behavior.

Jill continued to speak, but Mom never heard another word. She tried to focus her gaze on the garden, but instead of seeing the flowers, she saw only the pattern of raindrops on the windowpane. As she struggled to gain control of her feelings, her thoughts began to swirl in her head. Like fallen leaves surprised by a sudden gust of wind, they swooped and spiraled without direction.

*How can this be happening to me?* she thought. *How can one small child take away everything I've ever believed about myself?*

*Why doesn't anyone else see what I see?*

*Am I simply imagining things?*

*Am I the real reason behind Jonathan's problems?*

*Why can't I get anyone to understand me?*

*Why, oh why, do I feel so terribly alone?*

As these thoughts tapped out a jarring rhythm in her mind, Mom ran from the restaurant. She ran from her friend. But she couldn't run from the sadness that covered her like a dismal, gray cloud.

♥

A few days after Mom's lunch with Jill, Dad came home from work a little earlier than usual. As he walked in the front door, an angry scream broke through the sound of children's chatter. He followed the noise into the living room, where Mom and the three children were gathered around a lamp that lay broken at their feet.

"Damn you, Jonathan!" Mom shrieked. "How many times have I told you not to play ball in the house?"

She continued to scream at him, grabbing his

shirt and shaking him as she towered over his small body. Heightened by her rage, she made him appear even smaller and more helpless.

Dad stood in the doorway, watching them. He was shocked to see Mom's rage, and for a moment he could not move. He then rushed into the room, and for the first time his family was aware of his presence.

"Susan!" he boomed. "What's wrong with you? It's only a lamp, and it was obviously an accident. Let go of him—will you?"

Mom looked up suddenly, startled to see him. She released her grip on Jonathan's shirt and blinked several times, as if she had been in a daze. She thought briefly of her visit from Mr. North of Children's Protective Services, and a small shudder ran through her.

"Children, go to your rooms," Dad said, as he walked toward Mom and took her by the arm. As the children turned away, Dad led Mom to the sofa and sat down beside her.

"Susan, things are getting out of control," he said. "You have absolutely no patience with Jonathan, and it's not fair to him. Even Nick and Hayley are treating him badly, and it has to stop. I think we should *all* see a therapist this time—we've got to get our family back on track."

♥

The following week, Mom, Dad, Nicholas, Hayley, and Jonathan went to see Mr. Highland, a family

therapist. His office was large and airy, with over-stuffed chairs and lots of plants.

Everyone sat down, but no one in the room looked comfortable except Mr. Highland and Jonathan. Mom and Dad sat on the edge of their seats, and Nicholas and Hayley fidgeted constantly. Jonathan, however, seemed perfectly relaxed, as he settled into his chair and politely folded his hands in his lap.

Mr. Highland smiled pleasantly, then asked each of them what they thought the problem was in their family.

Dad said that Mom had no patience with Jonathan. Hayley said she wished that Jonathan had never come to live with them. Nicholas said he wished that Jonathan had never been born. Mom, however, said nothing at all. Instead she cried soft, silent tears.

When Mr. Highland asked Mom why she was sad, Jonathan immediately walked over to her and stood close beside her chair.

"I'm sorry, Mommy," he said sadly, before she could answer Mr. Highland. He placed his arm protectively around her shoulder, and without realizing it, she flinched at his touch.

Mr. Highland lit his pipe and leaned back in his chair.

"How long has it been since you and Susan have had a vacation from the children?" he asked Dad, changing the subject.

"Not for a while," Dad replied. "The children fight so much, it's awkward for us to ask someone to stay with them."

Mr. Highland puffed on his pipe, then continued to speak.

"It's clear to me that Susan needs a break from mothering for a while," he said. "Raising three children isn't easy, especially when one of them is a new member of the family. Getting away for a few days might be the best therapy.

"Why don't the two of you take a long weekend alone?" he went on. "Susan, the trip will give you a chance to unwind and regroup, and I'm sure you'll come back with a fresh outlook. You'll see that Jonathan isn't really a bad little boy. He's just sensitive to your feelings, and he's only trying to help you. He feels your frustration, and he's acting out that frustration. I'm sure that when you're more rested and relaxed, he'll be able to relax, too."

Mr. Highland turned to Jonathan then, and the little boy looked back at the therapist with a very grown-up expression on his face.

"Jonathan, while Mom and Dad are away, why don't you and Nicholas and Hayley think of something special that you can do for them?" he asked. "Maybe you could bake them a cake. Maybe make them a big 'Welcome Home' sign. I'm sure you can think of something fun to do that would be a nice surprise."

Jonathan smiled and nodded. Nicholas and Hayley smiled and nodded, too. But Jonathan's smile was edged with smugness, and only Mom noticed it.

Then Mr. Highland turned to Mom again.

"I believe that Nicholas and Hayley's anger

toward Jonathan is nothing more than their way of protecting you, Susan," he said. "They think that he's responsible for your sadness and stress, and they're simply defending you by attacking him. It's a perfectly normal reaction, and it will fade away as soon as you start feeling better about your ability to parent him."

Mom nodded, but did not speak right away. It was clear that the session was over, so she simply stood up and shook Mr. Highland's hand.

"Thank you for everything," she said, struggling with the words. But she didn't feel at all thankful. She didn't feel at all grateful. All she felt was the need to leave the office as quickly as possible.

She wanted to believe that a vacation would help, but it seemed to be such a simple solution. She still felt, deep in her heart, that there was a fundamental problem with Jonathan. But if no one else could see it—not even a professional thera-pist—perhaps she was wrong. Perhaps this really was *her* problem.

Conflicted by her shifting emotions, Mom hur-ried from the office as the rest of the family said their goodbyes. Alone in the hallway, she leaned against the wall to try to regain her composure. But the calmness she sought eluded her. She felt only confusion. Frustration. And fear.

♥

Within the next few days, Mom and Dad started making plans for their long weekend away. They decided to rent a house at the beach, and Jonathan, Nicholas, and Hayley would stay with their grand-parents.

Grammy and Grampy lived just a few miles away, in a warm, roomy cabin that sat beside a clear, blue lake. Grampy called it his retirement place—a former summer getaway that was now their home.

The children were very excited about their visit, and Mom smiled as she watched them pack. Their enthusiasm delighted her, and she actually began to hum as she packed her own things.

"It's good to see you this way," Dad said to her, as he pulled another suitcase from the closet. She smiled at him, feeling confident for the first time that all would work out well. Maybe Mr. Highland was right after all. Maybe—just maybe—all she really needed was a break from Jonathan for a while.

♥

The three days at the beach flew by quickly, as Mom and Dad filled their time with long walks, quiet talks, and endless searches through the tide pools. By the time Sunday afternoon arrived, they both had convinced themselves that Mr. Highland's solution was indeed the right one.

"I feel so much better now," Mom said to Dad, as she helped him load their bags in the car. But as she spoke the words, she felt a familiar tightening in her stomach.

*I feel good now,* she thought, *but how will I feel when I see Jonathan again? Has the problem really been solved, or have we merely avoided it for a few days?*

She glanced at her husband, who was locking the door to the beach house. He seemed truly at ease, and there was a relaxed air about him that she envied.

"For his sake," she decided, "I'm going to try to hold on to positive feelings. For the sake of our entire family, I hope he's right."

♥

Within a few hours they were pulling up to Grammy and Grampy's cabin, and the children rushed to greet them.

"Mom! Dad!" they shouted, as they hopped up and down beside the car. "Come see what we've done for you!"

Jonathan grabbed Mom by the hand, and together they all walked into the cabin. Jonathan led them into the living room, where a large, colorful banner ran the length of one wall.

"WELCOME HOME, MOM AND DAD!!" it read.

The lettering was done in red and blue paint, and the border was made up of dozens of small purple and orange handprints.

"Our handprints were Jonathan's idea," said Nicholas. "He thought it would make the banner more special to you."

"It's wonderful!" Dad said.

63

"It's the best surprise you could give us!" Mom added.

"And there's more! There's more!" Hayley cried, as she pointed to a slightly lopsided cake that stood in the center of the coffee table.

Mom and Dad smiled broadly, both pleased that the children had worked so hard on their surprises.

"They were absolute angels," Grammy said, as she gave Mom a warm hug. "You should be very proud of all of them. Jonathan, especially, was a wonderful little boy, and he planned most of this."

Mom returned Grammy's hug, as she looked lovingly at the children.

*Maybe,* she thought, *this family will turn out just fine.*

♥

**A**nd fine it was. Or so it appeared to be. The family spent lots of time together over the next couple of weeks, and they all seemed to enjoy their newfound happiness.

They rode their bikes, and Hayley managed without training wheels.

They went on nature hikes, and the children picked a few wildflowers to decorate their rooms.

They went to a craft fair, and Mom bought each of the children a small, carved wooden animal.

They played board games in the evening, and the house echoed with the sounds of their laughter.

Jonathan was having an especially good time. He knew that he had every member of the family under his control, and it was an intoxicating feeling.

Control was important to Jonathan, because with that control came a strong sense of power. As time passed, he was learning more and more about this family, but they didn't know him at all. This was precisely what Jonathan wanted, because closeness and understanding were a threat to him. He needed to keep everyone at a distance, because that was the only way he could feel safe.

♥

With each passing day, Mom felt more contented. Because she yearned so much for peace in the family, she held tightly to Jonathan's seemingly positive behaviors.

She didn't notice the singsong quality in his voice when he complimented her on a new sweater.

She didn't notice that he apologized to Hayley much too quickly when he ate the last of her favorite breakfast cereal.

She didn't notice how overeager he seemed when he offered to take Nick's turn at drying the dishes.

She didn't notice the phoniness he exhibited when he asked Dad to teach him how to fly fish.

She didn't notice that he never met her eyes when he spoke to her.

She didn't notice any of these things, because she didn't want to see these things.

♥

On Mom's birthday, the family went to dinner at their favorite Mexican restaurant. As they were seated around the table, Mom studied the children's faces.

In Hayley's face, she saw an excitement that reflected the day's festivities.

In Nick's face, she saw a budding maturity—a look that hinted at his growing independence.

In Jonathan's face, she saw a coldness that startled her. She quickly turned her gaze away, before the true meaning of his expression could penetrate her consciousness.

Dad ordered for all of them—a colorful array of spicy dishes that everyone enjoyed. They laughed and told stories all through dinner, and Mom thought it was one of the best birthday celebrations she'd had in a long time.

When it came time to leave the restaurant, Jonathan lingered at the counter by the cash register. When he was sure no one was looking, he grabbed a handful of matches and stuffed them in his pocket.

"Just what are you doing, young man?" a voice behind Jonathan boomed. He turned to see the manager, a large man with dark, brooding eyes.

"I . . . I . . . ," Jonathan stammered, caught off guard. At that moment, Dad walked back in, wondering where Jonathan had disappeared to.

Jonathan's mind began to race. He had to think
of an excuse, fast.

"I like the pretty pictures on the covers," he
said, indicating the various scenes of Mexico that
were depicted. "I thought my little sister would
especially like this one of the flowers," he continued, holding the matchbook up close to the manager's face.

"Well, I guess there's no harm done," the big man
said.

"Just put the matches back, Jonathan," Dad said.

Relieved to have talked his way out of the con-
frontation, Jonathan returned the matches to the
bowl on the countertop. No one ever knew that two
small books remained deep in his back pocket. And
no one ever knew that he would keep those matches
with him at all times.

♥

It was an early spring day when Jonathan slipped
out of bed just before the sun came up. The rest of
the family was still asleep, so he crept very quietly
through the house.

He peered into Nicholas's room, and saw Nick
sprawled across the bed with one leg flung on top of
the covers. His right arm was wrapped loosely
around a tattered bear, and Jonathan thought he
looked very peaceful. That thought made him angry,
so he left the room.

Next he peeked into Hayley's room. Her pink
little face poked out from the top of a fluffy, pink

comforter, and a doll in a pink dress lay beside her on the pillow. Jonathan could hear her soft breathing, and the gentle sound made his anger grow.

He sat on the floor in the hallway, letting the rage fill him. As he felt it swell, he thought about Nicholas and Hayley. Their parents wanted them, cared for them, loved them.

"They're better than me," Jonathan whispered to himself. "No one ever really wanted me."

He felt consumed by a heavy sadness and loneliness, but he quickly pushed the feelings away. He was far more comfortable with his rage, so he let it fill him once again.

He stood up and walked down the hall to his parents' room. Ever so quietly, he stepped inside. Mom was lying on her side with her back to Dad, and his hand rested lightly on her shoulder. They looked so content—just like Nicholas and Hayley—and Jonathan's anger grew bigger and bigger.

He tiptoed out of the room—careful not to make any noise—and ran out of the house. His anger pushed at him like a schoolyard bully, and Jonathan didn't know how to fight back.

He ran into the barn, and sat down on the damp ground just inside the door. Leaning against the wall beside him was a bag of charcoal that Dad used for barbecues, and on a small shelf just above his head, Jonathan could see a can of lighter fluid.

He jumped up suddenly and reached for the red and white can. He began to splash the fluid around

69

the barn, growing more and more excited as the smell of the fumes grew stronger.

He reached into the pocket of his jeans and pulled out his matches. Lighting one, he tossed it into an empty stall. Immediately, bright flames burst into the air. Jonathan dashed from the barn, pulling the door closed behind him.

♥

Not long afterward, Dad awoke, stretched, and climbed out of bed. He opened the window to let in the fresh air, but the smell of smoke came in instead.

He looked down and saw thick, gray smoke billowing from the barn. He could hear the frightened cries of the horses, and his heart began to pound. He hurried outside and raced to the burning building, quickly releasing the horses into the pasture.

He then rushed back to the house to call 911, and within minutes he could hear the sound of approaching fire engines. By now the rest of the family was awake, and they gathered around Dad to find out what was happening.

"It's okay," he began. "We're not in danger. There's a fire in the barn, and help is on the way."

But even though the fire engines arrived within minutes—even though the firefighters did all they could to put out the flames—the fire raged on.

Dad, Mom, Nicholas, Hayley, and Jonathan stood outside and watched the barn burn to the ground. The tears on their faces reflected the flames, but Jonathan's face reflected nothing at all.

♥

In time the fire was out, but very little was left of the barn. As the firefighters used their axes to tear down the remaining walls, the chief walked up to Dad.

"I'm sorry, Mr. Justice," he said. "There was nothing we could do to save the barn. Why don't you take your family back to the house, and we'll look around and see if we can figure out what caused the fire."

Dad nodded and led the family into the kitchen. Mom made hot chocolate—everyone's favorite—but it didn't cheer anyone up. Even when she plopped a fat marshmallow into each cup, no one spoke or smiled.

A knock at the kitchen door made them all look up. It was the fire chief, and he asked to speak to Dad privately.

Dad stepped outside into the cool morning air and closed the door behind him.

"I have some disturbing news, Mr. Justice," the chief began. "We found this just inside the barn door."

He held up the can of lighter fluid, which was charred from the flames. "The top was off and it was empty," he continued. "If this were used to start the fire, it would explain why the barn burned so quickly. It certainly looks like someone purposely started the fire."

"But why would anyone do such a thing?" Dad asked. But the fire chief had no answer.

"We'll investigate and let you know as soon as we

find something," he said, and Dad thanked him.

Dad went back into the house, walked through the kitchen, and slumped into his favorite living room chair. He buried his face in his hands, and he wasn't even aware that Jonathan had followed him into the room.

"Please don't be sad, Daddy," Jonathan said, as he walked toward the chair. "Everything will be all right—I promise."

As he said the words he suddenly wrapped his arms around his father's neck, and just as suddenly, Dad's weary eyes widened. He jumped out of his chair and roughly pushed Jonathan away. He walked to the window and stared out at the smoldering barn, his fists clenching and unclenching at his sides.

Jonathan couldn't figure out what was happening, so he returned to the kitchen and approached his mom.

"I think Dad needs you," he said. "He seems really upset."

Mom went into the living room where she found Dad still standing at the window.

"He did it!" he shouted, as Mom stood beside him. "He did it!" he repeated, pointing toward the kitchen.

Mom looked at him in surprise, not understanding.

"Jonathan started the fire," said Dad, his voice breaking in sorrow. "I could smell the lighter fluid on his hands."

♥

**M**om and Dad didn't know what to do. A part of them felt sorry for Jonathan, because he was a very troubled little boy. A part of them wanted to send Jonathan away, because he had brought them so much unhappiness. And a part of them wished they'd never adopted him, because now they felt they couldn't give him back.

They were confused. They were frustrated. And they needed help.

Mom decided to call an adoption support group. Jonathan's social worker had given her the phone number a long time ago, and she'd been carrying it in her wallet since then. It was worn and torn from the many times she'd reached for it, then put it back.

The phone was answered by a woman who said her name was Mrs. DeYoung. She had a kind and soothing voice, and it made Mom want to cry. She tried her best to hold back her tears while she explained to Mrs. DeYoung about Jonathan's behavior.

She told her about how Jonathan tried to get Nicholas and Hayley in trouble.

She told her about his attack on Polo.

She told her about his lying.

She told her about his stealing.

She told her about his ruined toys.

And she told her about the fire.

When she was finished, Mrs. DeYoung began to ask a series of questions.

"Does he act unusually charming?" she asked. Mom said yes.

"Does he have trouble looking you in the eye?" Mom said yes.

"Does he ask a lot of nonsense questions?"

74

Mom said yes.

"Does he seem to be unfeeling about hurting others?"

Mom said yes.

"But how do you know these things?" Mom asked her. "How could you possibly know?"

Mrs. DeYoung explained: "When a child, like Jonathan, is subjected to neglect and abandonment throughout his early years, he tends to behave in ways that are very controlling. This type of behavior prevents the child from getting too close to others, and the distance makes him feel safe. We call the problem attachment disorder—because the child didn't bond during infancy. The lack of bonding, or attachment, results when a child's basic needs aren't met, leading him to believe that he can't count on, or trust, anyone. Jonathan appears to have many of the warning signs."

A feeling of relief swept over Mom. All at once, the fears and concerns that she'd had for so long made perfect sense, and her questions spilled out like a waterfall.

"What can we do for him?" she asked Mrs. DeYoung. "Is it too late for him to learn to bond? Is there a place where we can take him for help?"

"There's a place in the mountains about eighty miles from here," said Mrs. DeYoung. "It's called the Alpine Attachment Center, and they can answer all of your questions. If you stop by my office, I'll give you some forms to fill out and mail to the center. Someone from there will call you to set up an appointment."

Mom took Mrs. DeYoung's address and thanked her. When she hung up the phone, she felt an emotion that she hadn't experienced in a long, long time. At last, she felt hope.

♥

**N**early two weeks had gone by when Mom received the phone call from Alpine. A therapist named Dr. Hawthorne was on the line, explaining that he had reviewed Jonathan's assessment forms and wanted to see him, probably for several sessions.

Mom felt a sudden freedom that was new to her. Her mind felt free. Her spirit felt free. But most important, her heart felt free.

She arranged to take Jonathan to the center the following Monday, then rushed to tell Dad the good news.

♥

**A**s soon as breakfast was finished on Monday morning, Mom and Dad packed the car with everything they would need for the remainder of the week. Grammy and Grampy had offered to stay with Nicholas and Hayley, and they arrived just as Jonathan was stashing a handful of caramels between the cushions of the back seat. He jumped out to greet them, relieved that no one had noticed what he was doing.

"We'll call you tonight after we've seen Dr. Hawthorne," Dad said, as he hugged Grammy and Grampy and kissed Nick and Hayley. When all the goodbyes were said, Jonathan and his parents climbed into the car and began the two-hour drive to the Alpine Attachment Center.

♥

Jonathan was excited. He had never been to the mountains before, and he thought it would be fun. He enjoyed meeting new therapists, so he thought that would be fun, too. He wondered if Dr. Hawthorne was anything like his other two counselors. As the scenery changed from the bright green of budding oak trees to the deep richness of stately evergreens, his excitement grew.

He began to ask lots of questions.

"How much further is it?" he asked.

"About fifty more miles," Dad replied.

"Why is the road so curvy?" he asked.

"Because we're in the mountains," Mom replied.

"Why are all the trees so tall? Why is that bird sitting on that branch? Why is the sun so bright?" he fired rapidly, one question right after the other.

"Settle down, Jonathan!" Dad warned, and the child was silent for a few minutes.

"Does Dr. Hawthorne smoke a pipe?" Jonathan began again.

"I don't know," Mom answered.

"Will he have toys to play with?" he continued.

"We don't know," Mom and Dad said in unison.

"What's he going to ask me?" Jonathan prodded.

"We don't know!" they exclaimed.

Jonathan didn't like the fact that his questions weren't answered. He wanted to know as much as he could about Dr. Hawthorne, and not knowing made him feel jittery and fidgety. He grabbed one of the caramels that he had stashed, and munched it greedily as he wondered about the mysterious Dr. Hawthorne.

♥

The rest of the trip was uneventful. Once, they stopped to use the rest room. And twice, Jonathan commented on some especially nasty road kill.

Soon they arrived at the Alpine Attachment Center. It was a large cedar building just up the hill from a small creek. Jonathan thought it would be fun to run down the hill and throw rocks in the rushing white water, but Mom and Dad led him into the front door of the building instead.

They were greeted by a short woman with curly red hair and freckles. She smiled brightly and asked them to have a seat while she notified Dr. Hawthorne that his new clients had arrived.

Within minutes, Dr. Hawthorne emerged from a door down the hall. He was tall, with dark brown hair and gold-rimmed glasses. He wore blue jeans and an open-collared plaid shirt, with the sleeves rolled up to his elbows.

First, he addressed Mom and Dad.

"You must be Susan and Dan Justice," he said, as he shook their hands warmly. "I hope your ride was a pleasant one."

Mom and Dad agreed that it was, and they commented briefly on the beautiful scenery. Dr.

Hawthorne then turned his attention to Jonathan.

"And this must be the little boy I've heard so much about," he said, as he bent down and peered over the top of his glasses. He put his hand on Jonathan's head, tilting it back so that Jonathan would look straight into his eyes. "I'm Brian Hawthorne, Jonathan," he said. "And I have a feeling we're going to get to know each other really well."

♥

Jonathan didn't say a word. He didn't want to look into Dr. Hawthorne's eyes, and he didn't want to be in this place. All he really wanted was another one of his caramels, but the car and the parking lot seemed miles away.

Dr. Hawthorne patted Jonathan on the head and told him to stay in the waiting room while he talked to Mom and Dad.

"We're going to be quite some time," he explained to Jonathan. "There are toys and books in the cabinet, so feel free to entertain yourself while we're gone."

Dr. Hawthorne led Mom and Dad down the hall to his office. Jonathan watched them go, staring nervously at their retreating backs until they disappeared behind a closed door.

♥

Mom and Dad settled into a pair of cream-colored leather chairs, and Dr. Hawthorne sat across from them. They reviewed Jonathan's history and

79

behaviors, and Dr. Hawthorne took notes while they talked. After nearly an hour, he took off his glasses and began to polish them with his handkerchief.

"As you know, Jonathan had many placements before he came to live with you," he began. "That fact, coupled with the neglect and abuse he suffered, makes it difficult for him to trust the closeness of loving parents. Jonathan's heart is hurting, and just like a child who has cut his finger, he is saying, 'Don't touch! It hurts too much.' Consequently, Jonathan's behavior is very controlling, and he keeps you either at a distance or superficially close. To touch his heart will cause him great pain."

Mom's eyes began to tear. "I always thought that if we just loved him enough he would come around," she said, trying not to weep.

"I imagine that at one time Jonathan had the capability to return love," Dr. Hawthorne replied. "But now, after all the rejections he's experienced, it's just too risky for him."

"So what can we do for him, doctor?" Dad asked, moving to the edge of his seat.

Dr. Hawthorne pocketed his handkerchief and put his glasses back on. He stretched his long legs out in front of him, and then he spoke.

"When I was in college, I took in a stray tomcat," he said. "He was young and full of himself. One night, he seemed very ill. He walked slowly, he wouldn't play, and he refused to eat. I noticed a large lump just under his jaw, and when I reached to examine it, he hissed and scratched me viciously.

81

"I felt I had to do something, so I quickly grabbed him by the back of the neck and turned him over. The lump was an abscess from a cat bite—obviously very painful. I removed the scab and squeezed the infection out of the wound. Then I applied antibiotic ointment and put him down. Within an hour, he ate. Later that night, he jumped on my lap and purred while I rubbed his chin.

"Jonathan is like that cat," Dr. Hawthorne continued. "But instead of a simple abscess, his whole heart is infected. He has scratched other families who have tried to get close to him, and he has scratched you. While others have sent him away, you have chosen to hang on. I admire your courage. If Jonathan is going to make it, it will be with people like you."

Mom and Dad looked at each other and smiled. They were both crying now.

"Helping Jonathan to heal will take strong therapy and strong parenting," Dr. Hawthorne said. "His symptoms are well-honed defenses that keep everyone at bay. We must help him break through these defenses so that he can feel his pain and begin to heal. Otherwise," he said softly, "Jonathan will never feel enough for others to get close to them or care about them, and his behaviors will become more dangerous."

"What needs to be done to help Jonathan break down his defenses?" Mom inquired.

Dr. Hawthorne picked up Jonathan's file and leaned forward, resting his elbows on his knees. Gesturing with the folder, he began to speak.

"Jonathan's defenses require a great deal of

control. In fact, when you look closely at his behaviors—his phony sincerity, his lying, his stealing, and especially his destructive patterns—you can begin to see how vitally important control is to Jonathan. He's a seven-year-old child who truly believes that he doesn't need parents to love and care for him. Quite the contrary, Jonathan thinks he must stay in charge to survive.

"I would like to help Jonathan by taking away his control," Dr. Hawthorne said, and he paused briefly before continuing.

"A baby who bonds to his mother in infancy willingly gives up control to her when he is distressed. Like this baby, Jonathan needs to learn that he, too, can give up control. He needs to learn that when he does, he will experience love and trust rather than abuse and abandonment.

"Because Jonathan developed his defenses in order to survive, he will not give up control freely. Therefore, I need to make sure right from the beginning that he's not allowed to manipulate the therapy. No conning. No lying. No false charm. To help ensure this, I'll take charge of him physically by holding him.

"Holding Jonathan is important for two reasons," Dr. Hawthorne went on. "First, when he's not in control he'll become distressed and angry—just like that cat—and I don't want him to hurt himself or me. Second, it's critical that I take control from him in a close and nurturing way, so that when the infection in his heart begins to come out, he can experience the love he so desperately needs."

"But won't you be doing this against his will?"

Dad asked, his brow furrowing as he posed the question.

Dr. Hawthorne grinned. "Absolutely," he stated simply.

"But aren't you saying that he won't have any choice?" Mom asked, her concern evident in her voice.

Dr. Hawthorne placed Jonathan's file on his desk and folded his hands.

"Children don't always have choices," he said. "Jonathan didn't choose to have his birth mom abuse and abandon him. When you've taken Nick or Hayley to the doctor for checkups or shots, did they have any choice?"

Mom and Dad exchanged looks of surprised recognition, then Mom smiled and directed her comments to Dr. Hawthorne.

"When Hayley was two she had a terrible ear infection, so I took her to the pediatrician. When he tried to examine her, she got so scared and angry that she screamed and wouldn't let him look in her ears. I had to hold her arms and legs just to let him get close, and it was even worse when he had to give her an injection."

Dr. Hawthorne nodded knowingly.

"I'm still not sure that holding him will make any difference," Dad said hesitantly. "Jonathan has already been seen by two therapists, and his behavior never changed. Besides, your methodology sounds so extreme."

Dr. Hawthorne leaned forward to answer, but before he said a word, Mom began to speak.

"Maybe it will take something extreme to get

through to Jonathan," she said, a note of desperation sounding in her voice. "At this point I'm prepared to try just about anything that might make a difference."

Dad glanced at Mom, then directed his question to Dr. Hawthorne. "Are you sure your type of therapy will work, doctor?" Dad asked.

"I'll be completely straightforward with you, Dan," Dr. Hawthorne answered. "Some children respond well to holding therapy; others have more finely tuned defenses, and resist it with every resource they have. If it seems clear to me that Jonathan won't respond, I'll stop right away."

Mom and Dad exchanged looks of concern, both wondering if their child would be one of the tough ones. There was a brief, uncomfortable silence, then Mom spoke up.

"What is our role in all of this?" she asked.

"After I spend some time alone with Jonathan, I'll have you come into the treatment room," Dr. Hawthorne responded. "I'll ask you to hold him for a while, and I'll show you how to do it. In time, he'll exhibit some real extremes of emotion. He'll probably go through a cycle of eruption and resolution— exploding in anger one minute, then calming down and becoming compliant the next. Just follow my lead, and try not to let your own emotions get in the way of his reactions.

"When most children experience this therapy, their defenses break down and they become susceptible to all kinds of input. Our goal is to recreate Jonathan's early vulnerability, and replace the abuse and abandonment with nurturing and love."

85

Dr. Hawthorne paused to let his words take effect, then continued. "Obviously, you've both been through a lot of pain with Jonathan. Yet here you are, willing to keep trying to help him. If I didn't believe that you were capable of providing the care and support that your son needs, I wouldn't even be suggesting the therapy."

As Mom and Dad listened to Dr. Hawthorne explain further details of the holding, an understanding and determination passed through them without a word.

"We'd like you to work with Jonathan," Dad said finally, knowing he was speaking for both of them. "Can you start today?"

"I can start right now," Dr. Hawthorne replied.

Then they all went back to the waiting room to get Jonathan.

♥

Jonathan had been waiting for a long, long time. As his anxiety grew so did his anger, and he fought to keep it locked in his secret place. When he saw his parents coming, he closed his book and forced a carefree smile.

"I'm sorry you had to wait so long, Jonathan," Mom said, as she put her hand on his shoulder. "But we've been learning so much about you from Dr. Hawthorne."

Jonathan's smile quickly faded. *How could he know anything about me?* he thought, as he looked from his mom to his dad to Dr. Hawthorne in search of the answer.

Before Jonathan had a chance to grab hold of the situation, Dr. Hawthorne stepped up to him. "Now it's your turn, Jonathan," he said. "Come with me."

But instead of heading toward the office where he had taken Mom and Dad, Dr. Hawthorne led Jonathan to the end of a long corridor and into a small room. There was a large green sofa along one wall, with rose-colored pillows propped up against the arms.

"Wait here—I'll be right back," said Dr. Hawthorne. He closed the door and motioned for Mom and Dad to join him in the room right next to the one where he had left Jonathan.

This room was dimly lit, with a television camera and monitor in one corner. There were three soft chairs, and in the wall was a large window. When Mom and Dad looked through it, they could see Jonathan sitting on the sofa in the room next door. He looked very anxious, and his eyes darted nervously around the room.

"Can he see us?" Mom whispered.

"No, this is a one-way mirror," said Dr. Hawthorne, as he tapped lightly on the glass. "And the rooms are soundproof, so you don't have to whisper."

He made sure that Mom and Dad were comfortable, then left to join Jonathan.

♥

When Dr. Hawthorne entered the room and closed the door, Jonathan immediately tried to take control of the situation by asking questions.

"Why is that big mirror there?" he asked, pointing to the wall. When Dr. Hawthorne didn't answer, Jonathan tried again. "Why is that microphone hanging from the ceiling?"

Dr. Hawthorne walked to the sofa, sat down, and placed Jonathan on his lap. The child willingly complied, because he knew that pretending to cooperate helped him to stay in charge.

"Jonathan, look at me," he said. "Are we here to talk about mirrors and microphones, or are we here to talk about you?"

"We're here to talk about me, I guess," Jonathan replied, frowning slightly.

"Good, then we can get started," Dr. Hawthorne said, as he took off his glasses. "Tell me, Jonathan, do you know why you're here?"

"It's because of the barn," Jonathan answered. "But I didn't do it! No one saw me!" he shouted.

"If someone were going to burn down a barn, Jonathan, what would he have to be feeling in his heart?"

"I don't know," whined Jonathan, as he begin to fidget in Dr. Hawthorne's lap. Things were not going the way he had planned. He felt his control slipping away, and the feeling frightened him.

"Look at me, Jonathan!" Dr. Hawthorne ordered sternly. "'I don't know' is not an answer. Today we'll be talking about four feelings—mad, sad, glad, and scared. Now which one of those feelings starts fires, Jonathan?"

"Maybe mad," came the soft reply.

"Very good," said Dr. Hawthorne, as he gently cradled Jonathan and lowered the child's head so it rested on a pillow. He leaned forward slightly so he could slide Jonathan's right hand behind his back. Straightening up, he brushed the boy's hair out of his eyes and began to speak.

"Jonathan, lots of things can happen to put mad in a boy's heart. I think some of those things happened to you."

Jonathan was frightened. He could feel his anger creeping out of his secret place. He had to do something *right now*.

"I don't know what you're talking about," Jonathan protested. "I don't have mad in my heart. I didn't start that fire!"

Dr. Hawthorne grinned. "You know what I like about you, Jonathan?" he asked. "When you lie, you look me right in the eye."

He bent down and kissed Jonathan lightly on the forehead.

Jonathan could contain his anger no longer. The defenses he'd always been able to rely on were no longer working, and he felt his control slipping further and further away. As his desperation grew, his eyes welled with tears and he began to yell.

"Let me go! Let me go *now*!"

Dr. Hawthorne quickly placed his hand over Jonathan's mouth. It was not a rough gesture, but the suddenness of the move startled the boy.

"How are you feeling about me right now?" Dr. Hawthorne demanded, lifting his hand from Jonathan's mouth.

89

"I know why you're called a psychotherapist!" Jonathan bellowed. "Because you're a psycho, that's why!"

Dr. Hawthorne let out a hearty laugh, which infuriated Jonathan. He struggled in the therapist's lap and began to shout again.

"I want my mom! I want to go home!" But Dr. Hawthorne ignored him, again putting his hand over the child's mouth.

"I want you to tell me how you're feeling about me," he repeated, as he bent down closer to Jonathan. "Mad, sad, glad, or scared?"

He lifted his hand again, and Jonathan screamed, "I'm mad at you!"

"Say it again."

"I'm mad at you!"

"Again!"

"I'M MAD AT YOU!" Jonathan shrieked. "I HATE YOU! I HATE YOU!" he roared, bursting into tears and trying to sit up. Dr. Hawthorne curled him to his chest, holding him tightly.

When Jonathan's sobs began to subside, Dr. Hawthorne put the child's head back on the pillow and spoke to him in a soft voice.

"You have a lot of mad in you, don't you, Jonathan?" he asked.

Jonathan was exhausted by his emotional outburst, and tears streamed down his face. He felt powerless, and he wished he could be anywhere else in the world but here. Reaching into the far corners of his resources, he decided to offer up a few morsels of truth in the hope that they might provide a quick end to the session. He nodded in agreement to Dr. Hawthorne's question.

"Enough mad to do lots of mad things, like setting the barn on fire?" Dr. Hawthorne continued.

"Yes," Jonathan whispered and closed his eyes in resignation.

"Thank you for being honest," Dr. Hawthorne said, as he gently kissed Jonathan on the forehead once again.

♥

*D*r. Hawthorne wasn't sure how far he would get with Jonathan during his first session, but since the child's defenses seemed to be down, he pressed on.

"Jonathan, this is a special room with thick walls. The mad in your heart can come out in this room, and no one will hear. Got it?"

"Got what?" Jonathan asked, hoping that feigning confusion would push Dr. Hawthorne away from his anger and his pain.

Dr. Hawthorne considered the child's question for a moment, smiled, and said in a soothing voice, "Jonathan, you've had a rough life. People have hurt you and left you. You've had to be your own boss, because you didn't have good bosses. But here, Jonathan, I'm the boss. And as a good boss, I can safely say that you're not stupid and neither am I. Now," he continued more sternly, "when I say 'got it,' I want you to say 'got it.' Got it?"

"Got it," Jonathan repeated in defeat.

"Good," Dr. Hawthorne said, pausing only slightly

before he pressed on. "Now if you had to guess, who would you say put the mad in your heart?"

"I did," Jonathan declared.

"Jonathan, you've had this mad in your heart for a long, long time—ever since you were a baby. Do you think babies put mad in their own hearts?"

"No, I guess not," Jonathan answered hesitantly.

"Do you think your adoptive parents put it there?" Dr. Hawthorne asked.

"No, they've been really nice to me," replied Jonathan.

"How about those boys at the receiving home?" Dr. Hawthorne pressed on. "The ones you said touched you in private places. Did they put the mad in your heart?"

Jonathan abruptly looked away from the therapist, and Dr. Hawthorne knew he would have to come back to this subject later.

"Tell me about your birth mom," he said, changing the direction of his questions. "How long has it been since you've seen her?"

Jonathan flinched. "It's been a really long time," he answered sadly. "The police came and took her away. They took her and that man—that man who touched me down there," he said, looking away again.

A tear slowly rolled down Jonathan's cheek. Dr. Hawthorne gently wiped it away with his fingertips, then asked, "If your tears could talk, Jonathan, what would they say?"

Jonathan could not get the image of his birth mother out of his mind. His anger began to give way to sorrow. His heart had been broken, and the memory hurt him so badly that he winced and swallowed hard.

"That I miss my mom!" Jonathan sobbed, unable to hide his feelings.

"Look at me and say it again—louder," Dr. Hawthorne ordered.

"I miss my mom!"

"Again."

"I miss my mom!"

"Once more!"

"I MISS MY MOMMY !" Jonathan screamed, as he erupted into loud, guttural crying.

Dr. Hawthorne again curled Jonathan to his chest and rocked him for a long time. And for a long time they worked on what Dr. Hawthorne called "getting the mad out."

♥

On a signal from Dr. Hawthorne, Mom and Dad came into the therapy room. Mom's makeup was smeared, and Dad's eyes were red and puffy.

Dr. Hawthorne directed them to sit side by side on the sofa, and he placed Jonathan on their laps. He then sat on a chair facing them.

"Jonathan, I want you to tell Mom and Dad what we've been talking about," prompted Dr. Hawthorne.

Jonathan looked at both of his parents, and he said, "We've been talking about the mad I have in my heart."

"And how did that mad get there?" asked Dr. Hawthorne.

"Because no one took very good care of me when

I was really little," Jonathan answered.

"And who do you act mad at a lot of the time?"

"Mom and Dad," the child replied, now finding it difficult to look at them.

"Do you treat them like you love them or hate them?" Dr. Hawthorne continued.

"Like I hate them," Jonathan answered quietly.

"Now I want you to look at them and tell them in a really loud voice," Dr. Hawthorne demanded.

Jonathan didn't respond. Instead, he closed his eyes and gritted his teeth. He hated being vulnerable with Dr. Hawthorne, but feeling this way with his adoptive parents was even worse. They had always been so kind to him, in spite of his efforts to keep them at a distance. Other families had sent him away for far less offensive behavior, yet this mom and dad were always willing to keep trying. That fact pleased him and frightened him at the same time. Love had caused him so much pain in his young life, and part of him hated his adoptive parents for getting so close to his heart. He felt confused. He felt conflicted. The seed of a new and different feeling was growing inside him, and he wasn't sure what to make of it. The feeling was guilt.

Dr. Hawthorne turned Jonathan's face toward his own. "Jonathan," he said, "you are very lucky to have been found by these parents. Considering that they have put up with your behavior all this time, I am fairly certain that they can handle the hate you have in your heart. Isn't that right, Mom and Dad?" he asked, nodding toward Susan and Dan.

"That's right!" Dad said, as he focused sharply

on Jonathan. "Jonathan, I want you to look at us
and get your hate out right now!"

Jonathan hesitated briefly, holding Dad's eyes as
he did so. There he saw a determination so strong
that he felt compelled to follow it.

"I treat you like I hate you!" Jonathan yelled,
addressing both his parents.

"Louder than that," encouraged Dr. Hawthorne.

"I treat you like I hate you!" Jonathan repeated,
raising his voice.

"Even louder!" Dr. Hawthorne boomed.

"I TREAT YOU LIKE I HATE YOU!" Jonathan bellowed,
crying miserably and choking on his sobs. "But I
don't hate you, Mom and Dad. I love you!"

Mom lifted Jonathan to her like a baby, and she
held him tightly while they rocked and cried. When
she finally lowered the boy's head to the pillow
again, Dr. Hawthorne gently turned Jonathan's face
toward his own so their eyes met.

"That was excellent work, Jonathan," he said.
"You're doing a great job of getting the mad out of
your heart. Now I want you to tell Mom and Dad
three things you've done that feel like hate."

Jonathan looked at the ceiling as if trying to
remember something that happened long ago.

"I can't think of *anything*," he replied, his voice
brimming with mock innocence as he averted his
eyes from Dr. Hawthorne's.

Mom and Dad laughed out loud, and Dr.
Hawthorne smiled. It was clear to them that
Jonathan was trying desperately to gain control. He
glared at the therapist, then abruptly changed his

expression from angry to angelic as he turned to his mother.

His attempt at manipulation was so transparent that Mom continued to laugh.

"Oh, Jonathan, you're so silly," she giggled, then kissed him lightly on the cheek.

Jonathan was close to panic. He had not felt so out of control since he watched his birth mom being led away in handcuffs by the police. His face turned bright red, and tears streamed out of his eyes with such force that Mom could feel the moisture on her own cheeks.

"YOU DON'T BELIEVE ME!" Jonathan howled. "SEE— YOU DON'T CARE ABOUT ME! YOU DON'T WANT ME! NOBODY WANTS ME!"

"Hold on tight," Dr. Hawthorne warned Mom and Dad. "Here it comes."

As if on cue, Jonathan began to struggle with a powerful effort. But Mom and Dad held him closely and tightly.

"LET ME GO!" Jonathan shrieked. "PLEEEASE LET ME GO!"

Instinctively, Mom lowered her lips to Jonathan's ear. In a voice just above a whisper, she began to soothe him.

"No, Jonathan," she said softly. "We love you too much to let you go." And then she cried.

♥

*D*ad, Mom, and Jonathan held each other for a long time. When Mom again lowered Jonathan's head to the pillow, he looked directly into her eyes and spoke.

"Mom, I broke Hayley's doll," he started. "I let the rabbit out of the hutch. And I stole your jewelry." As he said the words, more tears cascaded down his face.

Mom looked at him with kindness and warmth in her eyes.

"I know you did, honey," she said, "and now I understand why. Inside, you feel broken, too. Your mom set you free, and so much has been stolen from you in your young life."

She stroked his hair, now damp with the efforts of his earlier resistance.

"Now, Jonathan, please tell me where you hid my jewelry," Mom directed, a slight note of firmness entering her voice.

"They're in that old dresser in the attic," he admitted. "I hid lots of stuff there."

Feeling a strange sort of freedom from his confession, Jonathan then turned his attention to his father.

"Dad," he began hesitantly, "I . . . I burned down the barn." And with his words came a new flood of tears.

Jonathan looked into his father's eyes and found acceptance where he expected anger.

"I almost killed the horses," Jonathan said. "Why don't you hate me?"

Dad lifted Jonathan to him, putting his cheek next to his son's. "You have hot, fiery pain inside you, Jonathan," he answered. "We're going to help you get rid of it so you won't have to do those hateful things anymore."

Dad held Jonathan's head and looked into his eyes. "You're very important to us," he said. "You're more important to us than any old barn," he continued, his voice trembling with the intense emotion that he felt.

He turned to Mom, then, and kissed her tenderly. As parents and child held each other close, Dr. Hawthorne slipped quietly from the room.

♥

**W**hen the session was finally over, Mom, Dad, and Jonathan checked in at the Alpine Motor Lodge. Although Jonathan didn't want to talk about or even think about his session with Dr. Hawthorne, he felt somehow lighter and calmer. His mind wasn't so busy conjuring up ways to manipulate, and he wanted Mom and Dad close to him all afternoon.

That night, as he listened to his parents breathing slowly in the steady rhythm of sleep, Jonathan thought about how defenseless he felt when he wasn't in charge. He thought about how easily he had let Dr. Hawthorne break through to the secret place where he hid his feelings. Tomorrow would have to be different.

♥

**T**he next day, Dr. Hawthorne spent an hour talking to Mom and Dad, while Jonathan waited patiently in the play room.

"Jonathan was a joy to be around after yesterday's session," Mom said with a smile. "He was very affectionate, and he seemed genuinely happy."

"His eye contact was great, and we actually had fun together telling knock-knock jokes," Dad added, mirroring his wife's smile.

Dr. Hawthorne was pleased that Jonathan had responded well to the first therapy session. But while he wanted Susan and Dan to be encouraged by their son's progress, he did not want them to think that their problems were miraculously over.

"We must be careful of our expectations," he cautioned. "For the first seven years of his life, Jonathan has been forming a self-concept that governs the ways he sees himself fitting into the world. Until yesterday, Jonathan's behavior has matched his self-concept, in that he has controlled and manipulated others to keep them from getting too close to his heart.

"When behavior and self-concept match, we are in balance," Dr. Hawthorne continued. "But when behavior changes radically—as it did yesterday with Jonathan—self-concept is threatened, and that creates conflict. Today, Jonathan may very well try to show us that yesterday's behavior was the exception and not the rule. Our job will be to work with whatever Jonathan is willing to give us."

Which, for the first hour, wasn't much.

Jonathan lay in his parents' arms with his eyes tightly closed, repeating to himself, "I am the boss," over and over again.

He would not look at them.

101

But they were loving and patient.

He would not speak to them.

But they were loving and patient.

He tried to pinch them and bite them.

But they were loving and patient.

He tried everything that his hate and fear could make him do.

But still they remained loving and patient.

Jonathan was getting very tired. He wondered what it would take to get Mom and Dad to give up. Just then, as if reading Jonathan's thoughts, Dr. Hawthorne leaned over and spoke in the boy's ear.

"We know why you're scared, Jonathan, but don't worry. No matter how scared or sad or hateful you feel, Mom and Dad are going to love you and hold you close."

Jonathan glared at Dr. Hawthorne. In a voice icy with independence, he simply stated, "Leave me alone."

Dr. Hawthorne put his hand on top of Jonathan's head, and spoke in a voice that was barely a whisper.

"Being left alone has been the story of your life, Jonathan. And we're really sorry."

Jonathan turned to look at Mom and Dad. He saw love and compassion in their eyes, and he felt his resistance begin to soften. He cried as his mother kissed him tenderly on the cheek, as she gently wiped the tears and sweat from his face.

"I think that will be enough therapy for today," said Dr. Hawthorne. And again he left them alone.

For the remainder of the week, Jonathan had lots of therapy. Sometimes he worked hard at getting his hate out. And sometimes he worked hard at keeping it in.

♥

On the eve of his sixth therapy session, in a small bed at the motor lodge, Jonathan had a dream.

He was in a strange apartment in an old building. He was playing with a toy blue mail truck on a soiled linoleum floor. From where he sat, he could see his birth mom watching television in the next room.

Suddenly, a crack worked its way across the shabby floor, separating Jonathan from his mother. Hot flames and gray smoke shot through the crack and reached all the way to the ceiling.

Jonathan screamed for his mother, who turned slowly and gazed at him through the fire.

"Mommy, help me, help me!" Jonathan shouted through the roar of the flames.

But his mother looked so sad and tired, he knew she was helpless to do anything to save him.

Just then there was a banging at the kitchen door. The noise grew louder and louder until the door burst open. A big man with tall black boots and a red fireman's hat rushed into the room, quickly swooping Jonathan into his enormous arms. He turned and ran swiftly out the doorway, down a flight of stairs, and into the cold, dark night.

"Wait!" Jonathan cried, trying to wriggle from the fireman's grasp. "I have to see if my mom's all right!"

He continued to struggle, reaching back toward the building. But the fireman's grip was too strong, and Jonathan realized he could not get away.

"It's too dangerous for you to go back in there, son," the fireman said. "You could be seriously hurt."

Jonathan began to cry tears of immense sorrow and grief.

"Do you think she'll be okay?" he asked pleadingly, as he looked up at the fireman's face.

But it wasn't the fireman's face anymore. Now it was Dr. Hawthorne's face, and he looked back at Jonathan with sadness in his eyes.

"I don't know, Jonathan," he said softly. "I just don't know."

"Are you all right, honey?" he heard Dr. Hawthorne ask. But now it wasn't Dr. Hawthorne's voice. Now it was a sweet, familiar voice.

He opened his eyes and saw Mom's beautiful face, and she looked more like an Indian princess than ever before.

"You had a bad dream, sweetheart," she said, gently stroking his forehead.

"Oh, Mommy!" Jonathan cried, "it was awful!" And he willingly surrendered to her open arms. He shivered while she held him, and at last he drifted off to a peaceful sleep.

♥

The next morning, Jonathan told his parents all about his strange dream. They both looked sad as his tale unfolded, and they hugged him reassuringly.

When they returned to Dr. Hawthorne's office shortly after breakfast, Jonathan told the therapist,

too, about his dream. Dr. Hawthorne smiled knowingly, as he lifted Jonathan to his knee.

"You're beginning to feel your pain, Jonathan,"
he said. "It's very hard work, and sometimes it hurts
a lot." Jonathan nodded.

"You still have a lot of work to do," he continued,
"but getting started is the most difficult part. I think
you're a very brave young man, and I want you to
know that I'm proud of you." And then he gave
Jonathan a big hug.

Hearing Dr. Hawthorne's words filled Jonathan's
heart with joy. It was a new and strange and wonderful sensation, and Jonathan wanted it to last forever.
Impulsively, he threw his arms around Dr. Hawthorne, returning the man's hug with more genuine
feeling than he had ever known.

♥

As the months passed, Jonathan and his parents
made many trips back to Alpine for therapy. And Dr.
Hawthorne helped him to have his feelings.

He felt mad that his birth mom abandoned him.

He felt sad that he couldn't see her anymore.

He felt scared that Mom and Dad wouldn't want
to keep him.

And he felt glad when he realized that they loved
him and that he had a very special place in their hearts.

Dr. Hawthorne was right—the work was not
easy—especially when Jonathan was confronted
with his lies. Lies had always been his closest
friends, and he felt very protective of them. But as

105

his anger came out and he grew closer to his family, Jonathan realized that he didn't care so much about those old friends anymore. Dr. Hawthorne called this "coming clean."

Jonathan came clean on how he got Hayley in trouble with Mom's flowers.

He came clean on how he got Nick in trouble when they were sorting bottles.

He came clean on how he hurt Polo.

And he came clean on how he wrongfully accused Robert and Sam at the receiving home.

♥

Jonathan's therapy was a learning experience for the entire family.

Mom and Dad learned that their goals for Jonathan had to be different than their goals for Nicholas and Hayley. But they learned to accept Jonathan's limitations, just as they would accept the limitations of a child who couldn't walk. Or talk. Or see. They learned that Jonathan's willingness to be a real part of the family was a big accomplishment for him, and for that they were very, very grateful.

Nick and Hayley learned that even with the help of therapy, Jonathan would have good days and not-so-good days. Sometimes he would be a fun brother who joined in their games and laughed with them. Sometimes he would be a bullying brother who got mad at them for no reason at all. And sometimes he would be a quiet brother who went off by himself and seemed to enjoy just being alone with his thoughts.

106

But they learned to accept his many moods. They learned to accept his many behaviors. And they learned to love him no matter what.

Jonathan learned to get in touch with his feelings. He learned to let those feelings out of his secret place, because when they were out, they really didn't hurt so much after all.

He learned to talk about his feelings with Mom and Dad and to turn *to* them, not *against* them, when he had a problem to solve.

He learned to face his anger. He learned to face his sadness. And he learned to find joy in the simple acts of letting love in and giving love out.

But the most important lesson Jonathan learned was that he was not alone. Through the therapy, he came to realize that his adoptive parents had loved him—had cared about him—all along. He understood that he was worthy of that love. Like every other child in the world, he deserved security, stability, and the warmth of a nurturing family.

He learned that getting close to people could be a source of joy, rather than a source of fear.

He learned that opening up to others could help to ease his pain, rather than cause it.

And he learned that when a loving hand touched his heart, it brought him the greatest peace he had ever known.

♥

# EPILOGUE

Jonathan's intensive therapy with Dr. Hawthorne marked the beginning of a multi-phase healing process. Prior to the therapy, he was like a snowball rolling downhill—gathering momentum as he coursed destructively through life. Dr. Hawthorne succeeded in changing the direction of that momentum, but Jonathan's instinctive urge was to revert to his previous path. To keep this regression from occurring, there was a critical need for continuity following the intensive.

Both the home environment and the therapeutic environment worked in concert to ensure that the necessary continuity was maintained. Jonathan had ongoing weekly sessions with a therapist near home who was trained in attachment disorder. His mother and father employed specific parenting techniques that differed from those they used for Nicholas and Hayley.

While their birth children generally responded favorably to Mom and Dad's expectations of them, Jonathan did not. As eager as Nick and Hayley were to please their parents, Jonathan was often just the opposite.

Over time, Mom learned to take care of herself emotionally. She no longer tied her needs to expectations of her adopted son. She came to realize that Jonathan's success was his own responsibility, and her happiness did not depend on that success.

The intensive also provided therapeutic help for both parents. They became skilled at knowing when to address power struggles, and when to pass on them. They became experts at not taking his behavior personally. They joined a parents' support group and attended monthly meetings.

Jonathan's healing process was a long-term one. As the months went by, he had periods of regression when old habits seemed to be recreated spontaneously. In addition

to his weekly sessions, he sometimes saw his local therapist for crisis intervention. From time to time, the entire
family had sessions together. Occasionally, Jonathan vis-
ited Dr. Hawthorne for what the doctor affectionately called
a "tuneup."

But with ongoing therapy and proper parenting,
Jonathan's periods of negative behavior became less intense.
Of shorter duration. And further apart.

Control continued to be an issue for Jonathan, but it
was no longer tied to his survival. He learned to let go. He
learned to make compromises. And he learned to suppress
his impulses.

One winter morning—about a year after the intensive—
Jonathan awoke long before dawn. It was a school holiday,
and he knew it was much too early to get out of bed. So he
tossed. And he turned. But he could not get back to sleep.
He saw the first faint light of day slant across the walls of
his room. But still he could not get back to sleep. He heard
Dad get up and leave for work. But still he could not get
back to sleep. Finally, in frustration, he climbed out of bed.

He felt tired. He felt cranky. He felt mad. Mom and the
other children were still asleep, and Jonathan envied them.
He wandered aimlessly around the house, and eventually
stopped to think.

Suddenly inspired, he lit a fire in the wood stove. He
made a pot of coffee. He cooked scrambled eggs and toast
for breakfast, then woke Nicholas and Hayley. He served
his brother and sister breakfast, then cleaned up the kitchen
and washed the dishes all by himself. Next, he carried a
steaming mug of French roast into Mom's room and gently
called her name.

Mom sat up sleepily, surprised to see Jonathan standing there.

"It's only 7:00, sweetheart," she said, taking the coffee
that he offered her. "Sit down," she added, patting the place
beside her. "What's going on?"

Jonathan sat on the edge of the bed next to his mother.

"When I woke up this morning," he began, "I was in a

110

really bad mood. I wanted to run or scream or hit someone, and then I thought for a while. I realized that when I
do bad things, I feel bad. So maybe if I did good things, I'd
feel good.

"So I tried it. I did things that would make people happy.

"And you know what, Mom? It made me happy, too!"

# GLOSSARY

**ABUSE:** The infliction of physical or emotional harm resulting in confusion, helplessness, and breaks in ATTACHMENT.

**ADJUSTMENT REACTION:** A disorder in which maladaptive behaviors are manifested as a result of psycho-social stressors.

**ATTACHMENT:** In early childhood, the process of forming a trusting relationship with a PRIMARY CAREGIVER through dependence, the gratification of needs, and the building of trust.

**ATTACHMENT DISORDER:** A psychological disorder, resulting from early childhood trauma, that causes the child to mistrust significant others and to form defense mechanisms of highly controlling and confounding behaviors.

**BONDING:** The psycho-physiological connection, beginning in utero, between the infant and the mother.

**CORRECTIVE EMOTIONAL EXPERIENCE:** An experiential release of repressed emotion with resolution replacing pain and abandonment.

**HOLDING THERAPY:** A psychotherapeutic technique during which the child is cradled to ensure safety and to provide nurturing.

**INTENSIVE:** A course of treatment for ATTACHMENT-DISOR-DERED children, usually consisting of ten, three-hour sessions, designed to break through their defenses, allowing them to experience their emotions and to form trusting relationships.

**NEGLECT:** Inconsistency in providing for the primary physical and emotional needs of the child.

**PRIMARY CAREGIVER:** The person who provides for the vital physical and emotional needs of the child.

**THERAPEUTIC FOSTER PARENT:** A foster parent trained especially to provide corrective emotional experiences to the child who has experienced ABUSE and NEGLECT.

# SELECTED READING

**Ainsworth, Mary.** *Patterns of Attachment.* Hillsdale, NJ: Lawrence Erlbaum Associates, 1978.
Ainsworth investigates types of attachment in early childhood. She categorizes attachment problems and explores the origin and ramifications of each type.

**Bowlby, John.** *A Secure Base.* New York: Basic Books, 1988.
A pioneer in attachment, Bowlby has written many books and articles on the subject. In this, his latest book, Bowlby examines attachment and bonding in infancy and argues its importance in personality development.

**Clark, Jean Illsely, and Dawson, Connie.** *Growing Up Again.* San Francisco, CA: Harper & Row, 1989.
This parenting book is unique in that Dawson and Clark do not presume that all parents are the products of fully functioning families. *Growing Up Again* is not only a guide for parents in raising their children but also in reparenting themselves.

**Cline, Foster W., MD.** *Hope for High Risk and Rage Filled Children: Attachment Theory and Therapy.* Evergreen, CO: Evergreen Consultants in Human Behavior, 1991.
Written for parents and professionals, Dr. Cline expertly explains the theory of attachment disorder and its applications in parenting and therapeutic techniques.

**Cline, Foster W., MD, and Fay, Jim.** *Parenting with Love and Logic.* Colorado Springs, CO: Piñon Press, 1990.

In their no-nonsense approach to parenting, Cline and Fay teach parents how to raise responsible children through practice and logical consequences.

**Cline, Foster W., MD, and Fay, Jim.** *Parenting Teens with Love and Logic.* Colorado Springs, CO: Piñon Press, 1992.

Expanding on *Parenting with Love and Logic*, Cline and Fay explain how using logical and natural consequences rather than punishment will help teenagers learn to be responsible adults and enhance the parent/teen relationship.

**Gibson, William.** *Miracle Worker.* New York: Bantam Books/Perma, 1962.

Gibson narrates the story of Annie Sullivan's work with perhaps the most famous unattached child, Helen Keller.

**Magid, Ken, PhD, and McKelvey, Carole A.** *"High Risk" . . . Children Without a Conscience.* New York: Bantam Books, 1988.

This book is designed to educate the general public on the theory of attachment disorder, its social ramifications and how it is treated therapeutically.

**Samenow, Stanton E.** *Before It's Too Late.* New York: Times Books, 1991.

Samenow narrates his experiences working with sociopathic children and discusses what parents can do to help prevent this condition in their children.

**Verny, Thomas, and Kelly, John.** *The Secret Life of the Unborn Child.* New York: Dell Publishing, 1981.

A fascinating book about how attachment and

bonding occur (and sometimes do not) in the developing fetus. Verny also documents the psychological effects of childbirth.

**Welch, Martha G., MD.** *Holding Time.* New York: Simon and Schuster, 1988.

Dr. Welch explains how holding can enhance mother-child bonding and help children become happier, better behaved, and more self-confident.

# INFORMATION

For additional information on attachment disorder—or for a listing of therapists and support groups in your area— please contact:

ATTACH
2775 VillaCreek #240
Dallas, TX 75234
214/247-2329
Fax: 214/243-4210

Evergreen Consultants in Human Behavior
P.O. Box 2380
Evergreen, CO 80439
303/674-5503
Fax: 303/674-7665

# AUTHORS

LYNDA GIANFORTE MANSFIELD is an award-winning writer, working primarily in the arena of print and broadcast advertising. Her work has appeared in both national and international publications, and on radio and television stations throughout Northern California. She is also the adoptive mother of an attachment-disordered child.

CHRISTOPHER H. WALDMANN, MA, LPC, is in private practice with Evergreen Consultants in Human Behavior in Evergreen, Colorado. He has been working with attachment-disordered children and their families since 1983, and has been a consultant and therapeutic foster parent for The Attachment Center at Evergreen since 1985. He also conducts nationwide training sessions and workshops on attachment disorder for parents and professionals.